DIARY of a BUSKER

Volume I
The First Hundred Days

MARVIN B. NAYLOR

SKYLIGHT
PRESS

First published in Great Britain in 2018 by Skylight Press,
210 Brooklyn Road, Cheltenham, Glos GL51 8EA

Designed and typeset by Rebsie Fairholm
Publisher: Daniel Staniforth
Photographs by Marvin B. Naylor
Cover design by Rebsie Fairholm
Back cover photo by Duncan Paterson

Printed and bound in Great Britain by Lightning Source, Milton Keynes.

British Library Cataloguing in Publication Data:
A catalogue record for this book is available from the British Library.

ISBN 978-1-908011-89-3

www.skylightpress.co.uk

INTRODUCTION

In August 2010, I got the sack from the rock group I was playing in, due to the increasingly bad state of my hearing. I had been doing this for 30 years but it was apparent that my days playing loud music were over. I was at a loss and soon became desperate. Two months later I decided to take up busking, something I'd done very occasionally in the past, but now it was serious.

Being concerned that my 12-year-old son might get a ribbing from his schoolmates if they saw me in town with a bucket in front of me, I started my new profession a few safe miles away, in Southampton. Things didn't go well there, though – I made hardly any money, in fact barely enough to cover the train fare sometimes, and the weather was getting colder… and colder.

I did, however, find I was seldom lonely – there were always people coming up to me for a number of reasons: to talk about the weather (often) and – usually related to the first, to ask how I was getting on. Others would come up to chat about a song they'd just heard me playing – maybe it sparked a memory. In short, I was meeting many people I never would have met had I not been doing what I was doing. I decided to keep a diary of any interesting encounters and also my own observations 'out on the street'…

Marvin B. Naylor

The text in this edition is based on an ebook version, *Diary of a Busker: the First 100 Days*, edited by Nick Tann. Skylight Press would like to thank Nick for allowing us to use his text and for his assistance with this edition.

WINCHESTER HIGH STREET
BUSKING LOCATIONS

1. Opposite Bell's
2. Opp. O2
3. Opp. WH SMITHS
4. Opp. PHASE EIGHT
5. Opp. CLARKS
6. Opp. WHITTARDS
7. Opp. CLINTON CARDS
8. Opp. THE BODY SHOP

9. Opp. ERNEST JONES
10. Opp. VODAFONE
11. Corner of MARKS AND SPENCER
12. Outside DEBENHAMS
13. Opp. CARD FACTORY
14. Opp. ZOO JEWELLERS

15. Opp. REFLEX
16. Opp. OXFAM
17. Opp. MAISON BLANC
18. Opp. BUS STATION

N

TO KING ALFRED STATUE

BUS AND COACH STATION

THE STEPS
THE GUILDHALL
TOURIST INFORMATION OFFICE

COLEBROOK STREET
GOTHIC ARCH
WELLCOME GOSPEL HALL

BUSES

TO CATHEDRAL GROUNDS

NEXT
DEBENHAMS

MIDDLE BROOK STREET

MARKS AND SPENCER

FLOWER SELLER

HMV SHOP

TOILETS

UPPER BROOK STREET

VODAFONE

PEDESTRIAN BIT

MARKET STREET

PARCHMENT STREET

WH SMITHS

THE COVERED BIT

BAKERY

TO CATHEDRAL GROUNDS

ALLEYWAY

REAL PRAYER BOARD
ST. LAWRENCE CHURCH

PASTY SHOP

The Buttercross

To Westgate
The Westgate

DAY 1
Tuesday October 25th 2010
Southampton City Centre, Pitch D
Time: 1:40-2:00 pm

My first day busking in the city centre. I came prepared with my documents of authorisation and permission to use 'limited amplification' which I had to apply for via written request to Southampton Council. Just to use a tiny little amp. They then had to send me back the documents, dated at least eight days before the date I wanted to busk – what a palaver! After all that, I was there for only twenty minutes as it started raining almost straight away and became too cold to play – I have found twenty minutes is the limit when there is no sun – after that the right hand doesn't work.

A woman gave me £1 'for perseverance in the rain'.

Earnings: £1.62
Expenses: £5.50 (train fare from Winchester)

DAY 2
Wednesday October 27th 2010
Southampton City Centre, Pitch D
Time: 12:45-2:35pm

Played for almost two hours straight. It reminded me of when I did this on the London underground five years ago – you tend to play non-stop – literally. It gets to be almost like a trance! Not stopping, even for a minute, just in case somebody walks by who might throw in some money – maybe even a £2 coin. They won't if I'm not playing. No rain today.

Earnings: £15.16
Expenses: £5.50 (train fare)

DAY 3
Thursday October 28th 2010
Southampton City Centre, Pitch E
Time: 11:45-3:10pm

A long day – almost 3 hours of continuous playing. Had a few compliments – they're almost always from middle-to-old aged men! Occasionally, I'll be aware of some much younger blokes watching for a few minutes, at a safe distance away.

Met a lady from Düsseldorf out with her 1-year-old grandson who was clutching his Postman Pat and Mrs Goggins figures. I improvised the P. Pat melody on my guitar for him. The lady, Marika, is fifty-eight and chatted with me for a while. She had sat next to Rick Parfitt of 'the Quo' recently on a flight. Must have been 1st class, obviously. She has been living in England for a long time and her daughter wants her to stay but she's fed up with the racism – 'People use the 'N' word, you know, call me a Nazi.' She says she encounters this 'at all levels – poor people, rich people, in shops, everywhere.' 'Here in Southampton, you mean?' 'Yes, here.' I was amazed and quite shocked. (Apart from the fact that she wasn't even born when the war ended). I told her that, as a musician, I had been treated with the greatest hospitality in other countries, and in Germany in particular, but somehow never that well here in England. In fact quite a number of times, I've arrived at a gig having travelled hours and not even been offered a cup of tea. And then there's the dreaded 'dressing room situation' – invariably it's the men's toilet. If you're lucky, you might get the disabled toilet – at least they're usually pretty clean but more often than not it's the plain filthy gents – for four people to get changed in, with piss all over the floor.

Marika asked me about my accent and where I was from. When I told her I lived in Canada she said her uncle, who served in Rommel's Afrika Korps, was captured by the British and taken to Canada. He was only 17. She said he was treated very well. I told her I emigrated 27 years ago, to seek my fame and fortune, as it were. 'And now you are here? Begging?'

Earnings: £18.01
Expenses: £5.50 (train fare)

DAY 4   Friday October 29th 2010
               Southampton City Centre, Pitch E
               Time: 12:10-3:10pm

My last day at this pitch this week and possibly forever, as the earnings were so bad.

The day got off to a lousy start, as the minute I started playing – the usual 'opener', The Third Man – some guy came out of the Yorkshire Building Society office I was in front of and said 'I'm sorry, but I'll have to ask you to move on, as a couple of our customers were complaining that they could hear the busker louder than me, at the consultation desk, which is just inside the door.' I said I had a permit to busk here and asked if he wanted to see it. 'Yes please.' So I showed it to him, but said I'd turn down a bit.

Apparently, it wasn't him – he'd been told by his manager to tell me to move on. The thing is, the whole time I was there I swear I never saw anyone being consulted at this 'consultation' desk near the front window. I turned down – imperceptibly – and he never bothered me again!

Earnings: £8.77
Expenses: £5.50 (train fare)

DAY 5

Tuesday November 2nd 2010
Southampton City Centre, Pitch E
Time: 11:05-3pm

A long day. I arrived a bit earlier as I thought I'd make a bit more of this pitch, as it is right in the centre, opposite the mall entrance. Weather was dry, but the hands got too cold to play at about 1 o'clock, so I went in to the mall and sat on a bench next to two young Korean chaps who had laptops and were on Facebook the whole time I was there (almost an hour). Even as I came back from the toilets, they were still on it.

Back on the pitch, I meet Marika again. She tells me she's listened to an album I gave her of my original songs. I gave her the album free, as I felt sorry for her after hearing her experiences of racism!

'You sound very deep and sad, you know what I mean?'

'No, not really. Sad?'

'Yes, your song, For Francesca, very sad, yes?'

'Oh yeah, that one, maybe.'

Her grandson, George, was with her, again clutching his Postman Pat figures – Pat in the right hand, Mrs Goggins in the left, just as before.

Also met a lady in her 60s and her daughter. The lady used to be in a 60s girl group with two others called The Barleys, The Barneys, The Baileys, The Borleys, or something like that. Her daughter was going to audition for the X Factor TV 'talent' show currently popular.

'Well', said the daughter, 'if some of those idiots can get through...' These two were very amusing, but kept me from playing for about 20 minutes!

'What you need to do, Marvin, is learn a whole lot of Christmas songs 'cause of the Christmas market comin' up. People hear a song they know and they start singin' it and they love it! Anyway, you're smart lookin', you should be playin' in a wine bar down Oxford Street. See, *you've* made an effort to look smart, same as us (they were both really dolled up), not like this lot (indicating by a sweeping arm gesture, the rest of Southampton). Look at them, they don't care! Course, *we're* smart and have intelligence, but they, these people don't care. Thing is, these TV people like on the X Factor, they just want people who are stupid so they can tell them what to do. They don't want people like us. Anyway, where are you from?'

'Winchester.'

'Well, you should be busking there – they're all posh and got money. What you doin' down 'ere?'

'My partner has forbidden me from busking in Winchester.'

'Tell her you gotta make some money! ...'

After I had finished The Third Man (Chet Atkins arrangement/1960), some guy shouted 'Hey! Wasn't that from Spongebob Squarepants?'

Earnings: £10.51
Expenses: £5.50 (train fare)

DAY 6

Saturday November 6th 2010
Southampton City Centre, Pitch B
Time: 11:50-3:10pm

I was booked to play on Pitch A, which is an exposed position in front of the clock tower and in the middle of the pedestrian pavement. So, after exchanging greetings with the two jovial flower sellers (they'd certainly been on the 'pop', I could smell it) nearby: 'Do you play real guitar, are you good?' 'I'm better than some, not as good as some others,' I decided to return to Pitch B, where I'd been last week. While setting up, I was approached by a man, late 60s, who started talking about old music and recalled how he'd seen Count Basie's band with Ella Fitzgerald singing, at Carthage in 1967. He didn't have to pay, as he was involved with the company putting on the show. Then, some other guy came up asking me about my little Roland Cube amp and advice on what equipment to buy... 20 minutes later, the playing got off to a slow start, as did my collection; about 40 minutes on I finally get my first coin – a 50p piece in the gig bag. Hmm… the gig bag is too big, I'll have to get a hat. Had the usual twonkers and their usual tricks, like the 12-14-year-olds pretending to throw money, when, in fact their hands are empty. They like that one.

After an hour there's a voice beside me – 'Hey, let's take his money!' (What? – all of my 87p?). I look to my right and see a young guy wearing a Big Issue jacket. Then, switching his tiny attention to the vibrato bar on my guitar –

'What's that for?'

'Can you not talk to me – I can't talk and play at the same time.'

He kept on at me, so I said it again. 'Like I said, can you NOT TALK TO ME, I'M TRYING TO PLAY.'

'What you mean, can't you do them both, aren't you ambi – uh – dexterous?'

Money-wise, I thought I'd take a bit more on a Saturday, as there were thousands of people about. However, it seems thousands of people had other ideas.

Earnings: £12.27

Expenses: £5.50 (train fare)

DAY 7   **Friday December 10th 2010**
              Winchester High Street, opposite WH Smiths
              Time: 2:20-3:20pm

After a month of no busking, I decided to start again today. This was due partly to hearing a very loud noise, which turned out to be a guy playing an electric guitar over a taped backing band. I could hear him from half a mile away and thought it was a full band. I thought, well, I've tried Southampton, it didn't work – I'll try Winchester. After all, I live here and the expenses are zero.

I went home, got my Micro Cube and guitar, went back and set up opposite WH Smiths, just down from the Buttercross. Winchester's a small town and after 10 minutes someone said 'Nice sound, Marvin.' I looked up – it was my neighbour's partner/boyfriend. Then a few minutes later, Dave, a frequenter of the open mic nights at The Railway, walked by: 'Hey, that's not a 12-string!' He's only ever seen me with a 12-string at the open mics. Then a bit later, Frank the accordion player and his dog Kazoo. The dog was present, the accordion wasn't. I'd been chatting with him a few weeks ago, talking about busking in Southampton. I told him I played Chet Atkins arrangements, but was playing The James Bond Theme (my arrangement) at the time. I abruptly stopped and started Chet's arrangement of Mr. Sandman (from '54). Frank stopped by a bit later and told me about certain 'performers' – meaning the drunks who masquerade as buskers, who had been moved on in the past, '... but that was when Constable Murphy was in the force, he's left now.' Then, about the Salvation Army Band: 'After they do their bit playing together, they break off in twos and take over the whole street. I've sometimes knocked over one of their music stands – by mistake, of course.' As he walked off, he threw some change in my hat.

Apparently, Dave Brubeck was knighted this year. I was informed of this by a man walking by during a very cold attempt at Take 5.

Earnings: £10.12

DAY 8

**Monday December 13th 2010
Winchester High Street, opposite WH Smiths
Time: 12:20-1:20pm**

A very cold day – I thought I'd get there earlier than Friday – to get it over and done with! The sun was obviously not going to make an appearance during *my* appearance, and a drop of even 2 degrees made it almost impossible to play – after 15 minutes, I couldn't feel my left hand fingers. Even so, had a couple of men in their 60s come up and say they liked what I was playing. This happens, more often than not, after a rendition of The Theme From The Third Man, or The Harry Lime Theme. One – George – started talking, which meant I had to stop playing. He correctly identified my Third Man arrangement as being a 1960 Chet Atkins one. I'm impressed. He went away but I saw him hovering nearby, possibly waiting to hear it again. He wouldn't have to wait long; I play it every ten minutes!

Had to stop again, as it's just too cold, then George appears again, this time he's promised to get me some gigs (concerts, shows, performances – paid ones, hopefully). George 'dabbles in a bit of music' and says he can probably get me some work in London and Aldershot (?!)

Frank Williams and Kazoo

Later, as I was packing up, up comes Frank the accordion man with his dog Kazoo. I'd been chatting to him a few days before, when a lady came up and put a can of dog food in his accordion case. I mention this to him. 'She annoys me, although I smile at her. She's always putting a dog food can in there, and my dog doesn't like that stuff she puts in. It's a pain, 'cause sometimes I get a load of people giving me these cans, and they start getting heavy and I've got to cart them around with me. I end up taking them back to the shop.' I told Frank I'd got £7 today. 'Yeah? That's not bad for a Monday. You want to be here on Christmas Eve. Last year I picked up £100.'

Earnings: £7.26

DAY 9   Tuesday December 14th 2010
              Winchester High Street, opposite WH Smiths
              Time: 12:10-1:50pm

Another cold day – no sun at all. Very difficult to play more than 10 minutes and lost concentration several times – don't know if it was to do with the cold or my general mental state! Took a long time to make any money – £5 after an hour, so I played a longer stint than usual, but kept having to warm my hands in my pockets. Also, every time I looked up – I tend to keep my head down – I saw someone I knew, like the parents of my son's schoolmates. The local guitar shop owner passed by: 'Making your fortune, are you?' I recently had to sell a guitar I'd bought from him two years ago. He didn't give any money. Then, a bit later, his wife walked past – who *did*.

George from yesterday turned up – he's still 'working on getting some gigs...' He sat down on the bench opposite and I could hear him – bigging me up to the guy sitting next to him. I thought I'd made a pound more than I actually had – but on counting the money later on, I find someone's given me a euro – useless, as the banks won't take them.

Earnings: £6.86

DAY 10   **Wednesday December 15th 2010**
              Winchester High Street, 20 yards down from WH Smiths
              Time: 1:20-3:10pm

Another 1½ hour session, as I seemed to have more than the usual amount of people coming up and being friendly, dispensing humbling comments, usually concerning The Third Man arrangement. The trouble is, I'm finding it hard to take part in a conversation and play at the same time... and I'm not ambidextrous, as I pointed out to that Big Issue guy who was bothering me in Southampton. However, no one gives money to a non-playing busker, so I am eager to start up again. Then George turns up – his third appearance in as many days. This time he wants a photo of me to help publicise some gigs he's trying to arrange.

Later, a voice beside me –

'Hey, I've been listening to you, how much do you go for? I know a jazz club in Southampton. I run it, called Sunrise. Be honest, how much do you charge?'

'Oh, I don't know... I just played a wine bar for fifty pounds.' You idiot – that's cheap! – Why didn't you lie and say a hundred?

'Listen, yer really good, now, there's a lot of old people there, sometimes they look like they aren't listening, but they're just asleep – it's a rest home.' This was Pam, an American lady of about 85.

'Where are you from?' she says.

'You mean my accent? I lived in Canada for a while.'

Pam says she doesn't like Canada. She said she'd go and get some change for me. After an hour, I thought she'd forgotten, or gone back to her rest home, but she did come back and she did give me some change. She kept her word, which is something. I give Pam my card, so she can phone me about the rest home gig. Pam says she sometimes entertains the old folks with her ukulele – something I am quite looking forward to, if this comes off.

… I may tape a sign to my hat, saying 'NO FOREIGN COINS PLEASE', as I have had a couple chucked in today, including a 50 Forint coin. After research, I discovered this is from Hungary and worth about 26 US cents, but worthless to me, as no bank will take it…

Earnings: £11.22

… I'm still waiting to hear back from Pam. I'm fearing the worst.

DAY 11   **Friday December 17th 2010**
          Winchester High Street, opposite WH Smiths
          Time: 11:40-1:05pm

The coldest day yet and I wasn't looking forward to playing at all. But as it turned out, I was touched by the hand of human kindness. Half an hour into my session, with fingers so cold I couldn't feel the ends, a man about 65, who had been sitting on the bench opposite, came over – 'You play any jazz, anything that swings?' I don't play any jazz apart from Duck Baker's arrangement of Georgia On My Mind but that's slow – it doesn't really 'swing' as such, and I'd never busked it; but I mention it. He pulled out a £10 note and said I could have it if I played the song. I played it, but wasn't too happy, as I'd made a few mistakes and I'm not sure this guy was satisfied, so I quickly went into La Vie En Rose, which really does swing. He seemed happier with that, and I got the ten pounds. I thanked him most profusely – this amount is what I usually make in an hour. 'People want something cheerful, turn up, make it swing! By the way, I'm Paul, I'm Glen Miller's godson, you know!'

… A little later, a woman plonks a cup of coffee in front of me – 'To keep you warm.' Again, touched by the hand(s) of human kindness.

Earnings: £16.70 – thanks, Paul (Glen Miller's godson) – my goodness, whatever happened to Mr. Miller and that aeroplane…

DAY 12   Monday December 20th 2010
                Winchester High Street, opposite WH Smiths
                Time: 2:20-3:10pm

I wasn't going to go out because of the snow, but you never know with this busking lark what's going to happen. Turned out to be not bad at all, money-wise – £18.80 is a record profit, and for under an hour's playing. A very cold day with snow coming down all the time, turning to rain just before I packed up.

An acquaintance free day, apart from Frank the accordion man and Kazoo – not Yazoo, which is what I mistakenly called her today. Frank talked about his Saturday spot – 'Last Saturday before Christmas – always a good day. Picked up seventy quid.' As happens every time, I imagine, when one busker talks to another in the winter – the conversation comes around to the subject of how to keep the hands warm. Gloves, even fingerless ones, don't work when you're playing finger-style. The material in-between the fingers gets in the way. The busker who plays 'rawk' guitar over a 'rawk' backing can get away with it – he's playing one note at a time! So, how do you keep warm? Frank says, 'You go to the public toilets and put your hands under the hand dryer. Take a tip from an old pro, Marvin.' And with a knowing tap on the shoulder, he was off.

Earnings: £18.80

DAY 13   Tuesday December 21st 2010
                Winchester High Street, down a bit from WH Smiths
                Time: 1:30-2:30pm

Another cold day – they're all cold! And, like I should know by now, I never know what's going to happen with this busking lark – yesterday, over £18 taken but today not even £5 for the same time. I was sandwiched between Bob Jackson's rockabilly trio at the top of the high street – in front of the Christmas tree, and the Salvation Army Band at the bottom near the market. Still, must carry on ... until my amp spluttered and died – the batteries were dead; I'd forgot to pack the reserve ones and didn't have any money to buy some more. Time to admit defeat and go home. You win some...

Earnings: £4.22

DAY 14   Wednesday December 22nd 2010
                    Winchester High Street
                    1. **Down from WH Smiths. Time: 11:30-12:30**
                    2. **Opposite WH Smiths. Time: 2:20-3:50pm**

A 'double-header' – my first! I got to town earlier, as I wanted to finish earlier, but on arriving there were two young guys strumming Slade's 'Here it is Merry Christmas' or whatever it's called, opposite WH Smiths. The (by now) omnipresent Salvation Army players – a quartet this time – are near the Christmas market and Frank the accordion player is just setting up, too. And then there are all the charity and Big Issue people. Frank's a good guy, so I talked with him for a bit – about the cold, of course.

Played for an hour and made £5.42. Packed up and went to a coffee bar to warm up for an hour. I've noticed that toes take about an hour to warm up – much longer than the fingers – meaning the toes take longer to *warm* up, not that the toes are actually longer, length-wise, than the fingers. Something else I've discovered: wearing three pairs of socks is no warmer than wearing two pairs.

Returned for the second session opposite Smiths and took just under £10 for 1½ hours. Very cold. No notable approaches/conversations apart from a middle aged man who recognised The Third Man Theme, and noticing my red/frozen hands said, 'You need a young lady to warm those up for you.' I looked at his wife as if to say (jokingly, of course), 'What about you?' 'Oh, I'm not young!' she said.

Later on, I chatted to Rustin – a charity worker, who had exactly the same make and model of hearing-aid as I have. It's a small world, we both agreed.

Earnings: £14.63

DAY 15   Thursday December 23rd 2010
                    Winchester High Street, opposite WH Smiths
                    Time: 12:30-2pm

Got to the High Street at 11:30, but had to hang around for an hour before a spot became vacant – many buskers and beggars about. Salvation Army quartet in front of the Christmas tree, Rob – I found out his name – the American rock guitar guy sporting fingerless gloves (the lucky so and so), another Salvation Army sub-group and some guy sitting down hitting a very small drum – it could even be a lidded coffee cup – in an entirely random manner. The police have let the 'traditional' common or garden beggars stay where they are, as long as they are seen to be, ahem – 'playing' something – so they're not just sitting there begging.

Went to WH Smiths for a while, went to the church in the alleyway for a while, came back, watched Rob ... talked to Rob about the usual – cold hands. He says you can get some heat pads from the outdoor shop nearby. With me, I had two palm-sized heart shaped pads – one pink, one red, borrowed from a neighbour's 14-year-old daughter. You boil them at home, take them with you, then when you want them to work, you press the small silver oval shaped thing which is inside, some amazing chemical reaction takes place and they heat up. You can then warm your hands. But mine didn't work.

Rockin' Rob Berry at the Buttercross

Rob had sold only three albums; he usually sells ten – 'Don't know what it is today, people just wanna get where they're goin'...'

It really was cold. I couldn't play more than five minutes. I couldn't feel my thumb – not helped by the plastic thumbpick I use which cuts off the circulation anyway. I was playing by sight and sound, as I couldn't feel anything, very unnerving! I was going to make today a double-header but abandoned the idea – even now, six hours later, my thumb hasn't recovered.

Earnings: £8.02

P.S. I saw Frank busking on the corner of Marks & Spencer wearing what looked like an orange rubber jumpsuit – 'It keeps me warm but it's a bit sweaty.' What a guy.

DAY 16

Friday December 24th 2010
Winchester High Street, down from WH Smiths
Time: 1:15-4pm

A mild day, for once! So mild, in fact, that I was able to play for over 2½ hours with no more than three 5 minute breaks. My set-up time is no more than four minutes, including tuning up – then I'm off.

Ragtime Phillip, from yesterday, turned up after an hour, enquiring again about how to play the verses for Music To Watch Girls By – Chet Atkins' arrangement from '68, so I'm going over it slowly for him… 'E minor, descending, E♭, D, C♯, F♯7th, then a key change to A minor …' Fifteen minutes later and he's almost got it … he thinks.

Later, a woman comes up and says, 'I sing, you know – I could stand next to you and you'd get twice as much money.'

She starts singing 'The hills are alive… etc.'

'I could do that – what do you think?'

'I'd rather you didn't.'

'Well, I'll give you some change – I'm not giving these drug addicts anything. I used to work with them, you know.' Off she went.

So, the day before Christmas, and a lot of people about – I took over £30 – a lot for me. Thirty pounds and a used green Rizla packet that some guy threw in. I thought there might be a rolled up note – a message even, but… nothing. Some odd people about.

Earnings: £33.18

Marika and George

DAY 17   Wednesday December 29th 2010
            Winchester High Street, opposite WH Smiths
            Time: 12:10-3:10pm

Continuing mild weather = a long session! Played more or less non-stop, although the air was quite damp – my yellow guitar dusting cloth was more wet than dry after a while. Familiars such as Ragtime Phillip stopped to say hello; also Marika, the lady I met in Southampton, turned up. When I met her before, she was with her grandson. This time she was with her husband, who didn't speak to me. Perhaps he was German and didn't know any English.

Another familiar face, the guy who put the Rizla packet in my hat last week. He was standing behind me, for a few minutes, then came to the front and put a Ferrero Rocher chocolate in my hat, then went off, came back and put in one of those slim Corona cigarillos in the hat. So, no money, but something I can eat and smoke, although I would have preferred a Romeo y Juliet, Cohiba, Churchill or even a Jose L. Piedra. Then, finally, 20 minutes later, he's back again! This time plonking in front of me a cup of what might be, or might have been, coffee. But it's been half drunk and there are two round mothball sized things floating in it. I reckon they're picked onions. I take the chocolate and cigarillo home, but leave the mysterious drink behind. Weird, freakish people.

Earnings: £25.67

DAY 18   Thursday December 30th 2010
            Winchester High Street, down a bit from WH Smiths,
            opposite Santander
            Time: 1:30-4:05pm

Temperature similar to yesterday, but thankfully not as damp. The weather is always the prime concern in this 'game'… ALWAYS! Another mega-session with no breaks apart from standing up to stretch now and then. Lots of parents with young children – which is good, as the children see the busker – and today I'm the only one, therefore no dilution of attention/spondoolics! – The children stop, gawp at the strange sound coming from the strange man, parent gives coin to child, pushes sometimes scared child towards hat and hopefully the coin goes in the hat – the red Christmas hat for this time of year. Or, if they're very young, they'll just hold out their hand. They're sweet, the little ones!

Had the obligatory aged lady/gentleman voice their approval upon hearing The Third Man. Chatted to another busker – Guy, about not being able to play in loud rock groups because of hearing problems. This prompted Guy to say he has tinnitus in one ear.

'I can trump you, Guy! I've got it in both ears and have focal dystonia to boot!'

Earnings: £23.41

DAY 19   **Friday December 31st 2010**
             Winchester High Street, opposite Santander
             Time: 1:15-5:15pm

Set off to do an hour but ended up doing four. I'm worried about my Micro Cube amp – it started to crackle and splutter a bit around the two-hour mark. It happened the other day, but somehow repaired itself. Not today though. Even so, had a nice old lady ask if she could buy a CD. 'I could listen to you all day,' she said. Maybe she should talk to the girl at the desk at Clinton Cards. She *has* been listening to me all day. She might change her mind after hearing The Theme From The Third Man for the 50th time. Speaking of which, a 10-year-old boy came up and asked which film this was from – I think this was after rendition 36. I told him, he ran off and a couple of minutes later he comes back holding a £10 note – for me?! No. He'd won it from his dad – he'd given him the right answer! I think, really, he should have split it with me – I could have given him change from my hat. Parents should lead by example!

Later on… my amp keeps breaking down… it's not dead but definitely dying… a Spanish guy comes up and says he likes my sound.

'Well, thanks, but my amp's dying, I think.'

'Buy a new one,' he says.

'It's a lot of money, though.'

'Here, have this.' He produces a big silver coin.

'What's that?' I say.

'Look.' He holds it so I can see it for a second.

All I know is it's big and it's silver! Then he reaches down and takes a £2 coin from my hat as if to get some change for his coin. That's a bit cheeky.

'Whoa, wait a minute, what is this coin?' I say.

'Look, that's the bastard that killed Diana!' It's a Charles and Diana commemorative wedding coin from 1981. One side has the Queen; the other has the profiles of Prince Charles and Diana. He points to Charles.

'How much is it worth?' I ask.

'Shitless,' he says, and walks off.

Earnings: £46.48

P.S. A man came up, accompanied by his son – Horatio. It's Winchester all right.

DAY 20   **Sunday January 2nd 2011**
Winchester High Street
1. Down from WH Smiths near coffee café.
   Time: 2:00-3:40pm
2. Opposite WH Smiths. Time: 4:05-5pm

A split session, as I took only £7 for an hour and a half, and the constant cigarette smoke from the ashtray on top of the bin right next to me became unbearable. Got harassed by a gang of 15-year-olds. Their leader: 'Do you know any... (he says the names of about 10 bands I've never heard of)' – I say 'No' to all. He tries again – 'Know any Jimi Hendrix?' It's his lucky day and although he doesn't deserve it, he gets a 4 second burst of Purple Haze. Then, noticing my tan Samuel Windsor brogues – 'Hey, look at his shoes! Where did you get them?' I can't be bothered with this any more. 'I don't know, Shoe World.' Bored with me, they sloped off to annoy someone else. As they left, following their leader, the one at the back turned and said 'Nice sound, man.' He said it very quietly, so the rest wouldn't hear!

It was freezing cold today so I went to the church in the alleyway to warm up... then set up opposite Smiths and made twice as much as before in under an hour. Some familiar faces or 'the usual suspects', as I may start calling them. Dave from the open mics –

'Happy New Year, Marvin, hey, can I play a song on your guitar?'

'Um... OK.'

Dave proceeded to play a song he hadn't worked out.

At a few minutes past 5 o'clock, someone comes out of the bakery and yells 'PASTIES FOR A POUND!' to get rid of them. This is one of the daily rituals of the High Street that occurs always at the same time – I can set my watch to it. A few minutes after, Ragtime Phillip drops by and offers to buy me one – 'Yes, please' … but they were all gone! Typical.

Then, just before I pack up, I'm playing The Third Man for the last time – the last time *today*, that is, and a man with a green felt hat complete with feather comes up –

'I was in Vienna in 1946, you know. Now, do you know the other side of that record? Oh, what was it… The Café Mozart Waltz, that was it.'

Yes, I did know it, but not to play.

'Oh well, must be off to Sainsbury's now', he says.

Earnings: £22.06

DAY 21

Tuesday January 4th 2011
Winchester High Street, down from WH Smiths
Time: 2:15-3:15pm

Only an hour today – too cold! Started setting up half-way in between two young strummers who were opposite WH Smiths and the homeless guy at the other end, whacking his drum.

After a minute I hear a shout. I look around and see the homeless guy glaring at me. Was it him? I carry on and hear it again. I look at him again and this time he's flung his arms wide open – I suppose he thinks I've invaded his pitch. Well, he can come up and talk to me. All he has to do is stand up, pick up his small drum or cup or whatever and walk over. I, on the other hand, have almost finished my set-up and am not prepared to leave it to go over to *him*. I also do not respond to someone shouting to me. So there. Anyway, I'm at a safe distance from him, and it's not as if I'm interfering with him, musically speaking, as he is not actually 'playing' anything. He is hitting a small drum, coffee cup, etc, in an entirely random fashion. An idiot could do that. A dog could do that. So I reply with a similar sweeping arm gesture and say 'Yeah?' I then ignore him and finish setting up. When I look ten minutes later, he's gone, and I'm wondering if he's going to suddenly appear and hit me, or do something worse, so I'm looking around me while I'm playing. I'm not used to any 'aggro' as such, so I'm a bit tense for a while. I found out a bit later from someone that this guy moved to the alleyway, near the church.

Later, during La Vie En Rose, I hear someone whistling the tune behind me. I finish, look around and see a man.

'Was that you, whistling? I thought I was hearing things!'

'Yes!'

So we had a chat while he waited for his wife to come out of the health food shop – 'I'm 77 and I've just started playing the banjo...'

Earnings: £8.71

DAY 22   **Wednesday January 5th 2011**
Winchester High Street, opposite WH Smiths
Time: 1:25-3:10pm

Temperature is cold, but there's little wind, so I was able to play more or less non-stop the whole time. Proceedings were fairly uneventful – apart from the tramp playing her flute to Music To Watch Girls By. Well, she was playing her flute, but not playing Music To Watch Girls By...

Back home, Doll told me that one of her work colleagues said she'd seen me out busking and said to her 'Maybe he'd get more money if he got a whippet – isn't that what those sort of people have?' This really upset Doll. It goes to show how narrow-minded some people are. I'm a musician down on my luck, I'm not homeless and I'm not a tramp – I'm *always* clean shaven, with freshly ironed shirt (under thick jumper), knife edged centre-creased trousers and polished shoes.

Earnings: £19.14

DAY 23   **Saturday January 8th 2011**
Winchester High Street, opposite WH Smiths
Time: 1:35-5:05pm

Three and a half hours with only two short breaks of no more than 5 minutes. No other buskers about – the high street's mine, all mine! Even so, took no more than the usual £10 an hour. A funny thing, but no matter what day or time of day it is and no matter what amount of people are about, I never make more than this.

No one comes up to me for ages, then after my arrangement of The James Bond Theme, a voice from behind, 'Very good, Mr. Bond.' It's Frank the accordion player – or accordionist, I should really start to say – and the dog, Kazoo. A moment of excitement a few minutes later as Kazoo's mother turns up.

Later on, something sinister occurs. A man approaches. He looks like Stephen Hawking's double but without the high-tech wheelchair.

He starts a conversation, I carry on playing…

'People like pop music – you'd get more money if you played pop music.' I'm playing The Third Man.

'This *is* pop music – from 1949. Pop music, 1949 style,' I say, in defence.

He then says, 'I haven't got much money – I'm on benefits, you see. I have a formula, you know – if I hear someone whose playing leaves a lot to be desired, I'll give them 5p, or a bit more if they're a bit better, maybe 10p. Then, if I think they're incredible, I'll give them… 50p or even a pound. I've only got 7p, so I'll give you that, but it should be twice as much.'

So I'm worth 14p. Yes, I saw the 7p in his hand – a 5p coin and two pennies.

He then puts his hand right down, almost in my hat – a grey beret, now the Christmas hat's been retired, but instead of raising an empty hand, I can see he has more coins in it than he had a second ago. His hand is heading towards his pocket.

'Hey, you've got a fifty pence piece there!'

He gets defensive. 'What are you saying? Are you saying I should give you more?'

I think, I'm not getting into this here. I'm wasting time not playing. I'm gonna clock this guy and look out for him in the future.

About 55, looks like a wheelchair-less Stephen Hawking…

Earnings: £34.66 (Should be about £2 more.)

DAY 24   Monday January 10th 2011
               Winchester High Street, down a bit from WH Smiths
               Time: 12:35-2:50pm

A cold, windy (making it even colder – VERY colder!) and depressing day. I took just over £14 for 2½ hours of non-stop playing. Nothing to report apart from getting three £2 coins and a man who said, 'Every time I walk by, you're playing that!' a reference to my endless playing – and refinement of execution, I like to think – of The Third Man Theme. I gave the only reply suitable under these circumstances – 'It's the only song I know.'

Earnings: £14.09

DAY 25   Tuesday January 11th 2011
               Winchester High Street
               1. Just down from WH Smiths, Time: 11:15-1:45pm
               2. Opposite WH Smiths, Time: 3:30-5:05pm

A double-header, with a break in between where I went home and had some lunch. An old man comes up during The Third Man (naturally) –

'I recognise that – The Third Man. That's a nice guitar. I don't know if you remember, but before the war (I don't look THAT old… surely) a Gibson guitar was a hundred pounds.'

'Really? But that was a lot of money, wasn't it?' (It is now!)

'Yes, do you read the notes, you know, on paper, or do you learn from ear?'

'It depends how difficult something is – both, I suppose.'

'I have difficulty seeing,' he said, which relieved me somewhat – maybe I don't look over 80 after all. '… so I use this…' He produces a huge magnifying glass. 'But, you see, how can I use it?' He indicates by arm movements the impossibility of playing a guitar while holding a magnifying glass. 'I have a problem with this eye (points to eye), I've just had an injection at the hospital. There's nothing they can do, though – it's age. I'm 96 – my birthday is on January the 30th.'

'Well, come by then and I'll play you a song for your birthday!'

Later on… two men in their 20s walk by, one with a large scar on his cheek. 'Hey, we're trying to settle an argument – who did We Gotta Get Out Of This Place first – The Stranglers or The Animals?'

'The Animals, in 1964, I think.'

'That's great, man, thanks!' Off they went.

A bit later... Ragtime Phillip pops by for another quick lesson on how to play Music To Watch Girls By. He's getting it, he thinks. ... And much later... I'm playing La Vie En Rose to the delight of a French lady sitting on the bench opposite. She's wearing a full-length burgundy coat. She comes up and sings the melody right in my ear – in a different key to the one I'm playing in! At the end, she returns to her seat – and not before time! She's joined by Jeremy, a well spoken 60-odd-year-old, who often chats with me. They both clap vigorously after every tune for the next half hour. Cheers!

It's closing time at the pasty shop, and they're going cheap – £1. A lady – 'Would you like me to buy you a pasty, or would you like the money instead?'

I look at what's in my hat – I've been there an hour and a half, but there's less than £10.

'Thanks for the offer of the pasty – I'll have the money instead, if you don't mind.'

A minute later, a pasty shop girl comes out. 'I thought I better warn you, I'm gonna dump a bucket of water out here soon, and it's gonna go down there... ' She points to the drain right near me. Time to go.

Earnings: 1st session: £17.74. 2nd session: £10.59.
Total: £28.33.

DAY 26   **Thursday January 13th 2011**
               Winchester High Street, opposite WH Smiths
               Time: 2:25-3:35pm

Not too cold, but wet and clammy so I had great difficulty playing, as the hands sort of stuck to the strings. Made nothing until I started playing The Third Man, then four pound coins in five minutes, from four ladies in their 70s (separate – not in a group). I'm a bit concerned about what I'm going to do when all the aged people who remember this song – 'brings back memories', said the first old lady – are no longer here. I don't mean no longer here in Winchester, I mean no longer anywhere! But people are living longer, so I reckon I'll be all right for a bit – but how much longer am I going to be doing this for?

Still, I feel somewhat guilty – even parasitic – at times. I mean, I'd get practically nothing if it weren't for that one song! Maybe I should donate some of my money to the Anton Karas Estate.

Earnings: £10.05

DAY 27
Saturday January 15th 2011
Greenwich Market, London
Time: 1:30-6:45pm

A long day – the longest yet, and in a new location. I had arranged to visit my old mate Gary* at his flat in Greenwich, south London, so he could record me playing a selection of busking favourites for a promotional CD to send around in an effort to get some decent work. This was in the morning. Afterwards, he had arranged for me to do a spot of busking in the covered market nearby, so I could make my train fare back, with any luck. I was grateful to him for arranging for permission, and clearing it with the relevant authorities, because, in London, you need at least two signed medical forms, and permission from the council, if you want to stand in a spot on the pavement no bigger than 4" x 4" for more than 1 second.

'You'll make your train fare back easily, King.'**

I set up in between the market stalls and the Coach and Horses public house. A rather confined spot, as it was right in a narrow thoroughfare, and the head of my guitar kept getting in the way of people. However, I made the train fare back in just over an hour, and it wasn't cold and windy, for once. While I was playing, Gary and Loren Scott*** were in the outside seating area of the pub, busy keeping an eye on me and sampling the local beverage.

'Why don't you move over here, just in front of the pub – see how it goes, King, you might make more. You can always move back.'

So, five minutes later, I'm doing it all again, twenty feet from where I was. I wasn't sure about this – the takings weren't quite as much as the other place. I spoke to Gary of my concern.

* Gary Brady – talented musician, producer – film and music, animator, raconteur, experienced traveller, diarist and professional scouser. Tall and big-boned.
** King – King of Freaks. Origin unknown.
*** Local musician, artist and animator.

'Don't worry, King, we'll go round with the hat' – "we" being Gary, Loren and Julia – a lady in her 50s and a friend of Gary's who was dancing around and enjoying the refreshments, somewhat liberally.

So, here I was for the next hour… and the next hour… and the next hour and finally, the next hour. Halfway through the proceedings, the trio – Gary, Loren and Julia, were joined by Gordon the Hairdresser and The Kwaff.* The hat got passed around and the takings doubled. It was a good idea. Mind, if a 6'3", hoodie-wearing hulk in an advanced state of inebriation came up to *me* holding out a hat and more or less demanding I put something in it, I think I would give generously. I wouldn't say no. Definitely not. Sometimes I need someone like that. Hmm… Yes – for those of us who are somewhat backward in coming forward, we are eternally grateful for those who are *never* backward in coming forward. It is these people we meeker ones depend on for our survival.

After five hours of hearing my own playing, I'd had enough. Gary had been carrying out hourly spot checks on the hat and announced/ predicted well before the end 'There's at least a ton in here. I told you I'd get you a ton, King!' And he did. Afterwards, we relaxed, or rather, I began to relax, while Gary and Friends continued relaxing in the time-honoured English fashion. Gordon the Hairdresser bought me a fine measure of Cognac and I lit up a Jose L. Piedra cigar, sent to me by my brother in Toronto.

I was really grateful to Gary, without whom… and Loren, for her inimitable presence, and also Julia, for helping with the collection and purchasing for me a bottle of Bellefontaine Cabernet Sauvignon 2008 – 'with rich, herbaceous fruit flavours and a round structured finish', which kept me company on my train journey back to Winchester. A memorable and profitable day… for once.

Earnings: £106.76
Expenses: £21.20

---

* Kwaff: Geoff Glen – an old friend who has more knowledge and appreciation of 1960s/1970s music and fashion than just about anyone else. Kwaff – a reference to his hairstyle – corruption of quiff.

DAY 28   Tuesday January 18th 2011
              Winchester High Street, corner of Marks & Spencer
              Time: 4:30-5:40pm

A late session. I couldn't establish myself at the usual places – opposite WH Smiths or Clinton Cards, both along The Pentice, the covered stretch of the high street – as a youngster was vigorously strumming away and belting it out.

'You here to perform?' he said.

'Yep,' I said, 'but carry on, bud.' He'd been there 20 minutes.

'You might try down near the statue (King Alfred), or anywhere where you can't hear me.'

In other words, nowhere. I should pin a notice up here – ATTENTION LOUD BUSKERS: IF ON ARRIVAL THERE ARE NO OTHER BUSKERS ALONG THIS STRETCH DO NOT, REPEAT, DO NOT SET UP HALFWAY DOWN AS YOU WILL BE EASILY HEARD AT EITHER END THUS PREVENTING ANYONE ELSE FROM PLAYING. SET UP AT ONE OF THE ENDS. PS: AND DON'T BE SO LOUD.

After wandering about for half an hour, I finally built up the courage to try out a new pitch – the corner of Marks & Spencer, where I've seen Frank many times. It's quite an exposed spot and very noisy due to a bus stop just around the corner. It got more noisy too, as the minute, no – the second I started to play, I was drowned out by workmen drilling in a shop opposite me, next to the flower seller. It went on the whole time I was there. Quite a cacophony I imagine – buses every five minutes, the drilling and The Theme From The Third Man all rolled into one. Still, better make the most of it.

I had a guy stand in front of me for ten minutes while playing TTM. At the end he says, 'Do you know any Bruce Springsteen?' which is what comes to mind, obviously, upon hearing someone playing a theme from a 1949 film set in bombed-out Vienna.

I replied, 'No, but there's a guy up the road who might be able to help you out.' Silly man.

Earnings: £12.86

DAY 29   Wednesday January 19th 2011
               Winchester High Street, corner of Marks & Spencer
               Time: 1:45-3:45pm

I say a quick passing hello to Frank, who's accordion-ing it up opposite
WH Smiths, and set up at the same place as last night. I've been playing
a few minutes, then a loud voice – 'WHAT ARE YOU GOING TO
PLAY FOR ME TODAY?'

A man, mid-sixties, bald-headed, hefty.

'Do you know Mr. Sandman?' I say.

'NO!'

'What about La Vie En Rose?'

'AH YES! AND I KNOW THE FRENCH WORDS!'

No sooner said, he launches into the song, and sure enough, he knows
the French words. He's belting it out, all right. He's singing it quite well,
although he's missing out the gaps, the breathing spaces at the end of
each line, and in doing so he's making the melody one continuous line.
He certainly has an individual approach to the arrangement. I'm just
getting the hang of some of the more idiosyncratic, finer points of his
'style' when he suddenly walks off, mid-song. Still singing at the top of
his voice. It's hilarious – loads of people are smiling. In a way, I admire
someone who can do something like that and not give a damn what
anyone might think.

Later on… a woman gives me a pound and asks me if I have a DVD
player. 'I've got a DVD of a friend who died for twenty minutes and then
came back to life, it's here, you can have it – no money.' …

Another woman, about 70, says, 'You're very talented; how old are
you, by the way?'

'I'm forty-eight.'

She looks at me. 'Your hair's very grey for your age, isn't it? How old
do you think I am?' Too old to sleep with me, you cheeky old lady!

Then from afar, a familiar voice, quiet, but getting louder as it makes
its way back towards me, it's that man again – or ITMA, as they used to
say in the war. This time he's singing to the Spanish piece I'm doing.

'You've got a good voice, haven't you?' I say.

'Well, when my benefit didn't come through, I was singing outside
Nero's. You know, singing for my breakfast. I got SEVEN POUNDS in
FIFTEEN MINUTES!'

'That's good,' I say.

'YES! Then I stood outside later and I was singing for my lunch and I got some money for my lunch, in one of the Nero coffee cups, you know. Then, later on, I was, what do you call it – singing for my supper! HA! HA! 'Cause I'm not going to beg, you know.'

I asked his name – Maurice. I bumped into him the next day in Sainsbury's, singing his way around there.

Earnings: £19.00

DAY 30   **Wednesday January 20th 2011**
         Winchester High Street
         1. Opposite WH Smiths. Time: 3:15-4:50pm
         2. Corner of Marks & Spencer. Time: 5:05-5:40pm

Another double-header, as the first session took so little money – £6 in an hour and a half. And I was robbed, again. A young guy walks past, doesn't look at me, doesn't stop or slow down as he puts his hand down into my hat and I hear the change rattle. Where there were two-pound coins, now there is one. He didn't look at me – a dead giveaway. Subhuman scum! Ragtime Phillip returns once more for a chat and another lesson on how to play the opening of Music To Watch Girls By. This spot's rubbish! – Six quid in an hour and a half! – I have to go somewhere else – I always promise myself never to go home with less than ten pounds. It turned out to be a good decision as I collected almost £7 in thirty-five minutes.

A woman comes up. She manages a charity shop in town and wants to know if I'd be willing to play for a couple of hours for the re-opening, after the refit.

'It's all for charity, we'll put the collection box in front of you. We can't pay you but we'll give you a meal.'

Oh dear, here we go again. I'm a musician a bit down on my luck. I've got food! I'm not homeless! So we're discussing all this – although having been out in the cold for a few hours, my thought process is not working 100% and I'm finding it difficult to converse – when suddenly she shouts 'Oh God, there's my bus!' and is gone.

Earnings: £12.79

DAY 31   **Thursday January 25th 2011**
              Winchester High Street, opposite WH Smiths
              Time: 1:45-3:15pm

Played for an hour and a half with a four-minute break after the hour, during which I counted the money – just under £10. So far so good, but made nothing over the next half hour. It then started raining, so I came home, but not before a sinister occurrence. A while back, I was robbed by a Stephen Hawking lookalike. Now, I'm playing, I've got my head down, concentrating… I sense someone approaching. I look up and it's the same guy – the thief! When he sees my face, he stops, turns around and hobbles away. (What he doesn't have is a conscience, what he does have is a leg disability.) So there he goes, disappearing up the street – a guilty man if I ever saw one. I was thinking – what was he about to do before he recognised me as a recent victim? Was he going to take my hat? Did he think I was someone else – someone he hadn't robbed yet?

Earnings: £9.56

DAY 32   **Thursday January 27th 2011**
              Winchester High Street, opposite WH Smiths
              Time: 1:00-2:30pm

It really is getting cold! – The fingers get red, the hands turn purple, the breaks are becoming longer, and the playing time is becoming shorter. It's an exponential growth curve!

During a break, a very old lady is ambling towards me – she's attempting to manoeuvre her walking frame and, at the same time, fiddling around with her purse. Will she give me some money? I'm not even playing. That will be a first.

'I give money to buskers, I don't give money to BEGGARS!' she emphasizes the word, and very loudly.

'Please let me play something for you,' I say, or I *would* have felt like a beggar.

'I'm deaf.'

Yes, and I've just seen a badge on her coat which says 'PLEASE SPEAK CLEARLY, I LIP READ.'

'Oh, OK.' Then, speaking very slowly and louder than normal – the way the English do with village idiots and foreigners – I say 'I – WILL – PLAY – THE – THIRD – MAN – FOR – YOU.'

So I start playing, and she's nodding her head to the rhythm, which she can't hear, surely! Maybe she's getting the beat from watching my hand moving or maybe I'm shivering in time.

I play TTM more than usual today – there are no fast bits so it's one of the easier ones to play when it's cold. A man younger than me comes up and says 'I can't believe you played that – it's my favourite song!' We exchange Third Man stories – his: about Anton Karas being a pretty wild character, always disappearing from the film set. Mine: how the director, Carol Reed, had to get him to record the music twice as the first recording, put directly onto the film tape, was destroyed in a fire.

Then, the best part of the day and one of the best moments of my life… It's That (Third) Man Again, and there is a guy, late 20s – early 30s, sitting on the bench opposite, eating a packed lunch and tapping his foot to the tune. This pleases me. I finish playing, he gets up, comes over and says this:

'You know, you made me smile just then, and I never do that – my life is so bloody awful. You made me smile, that never happens with you lot. But you entertained me. You made me smile.' He puts a £2 coin in my hat.

I don't know what to say. 'I'm sorry, I hope it gets better soon. What's your name?'

'It doesn't matter,' he says, and walks off.

Earnings: £19.30

DAY 33   **Friday January 28th 2011**
               Winchester High Street, opposite WH Smiths
               Time: 1:05-6:45pm

Freezing cold with a steady wind, like yesterday, but I could only stand an hour and picked up virtually no money – just over £2. Even so, I managed to squeeze in The Third Man a few times. A man comes up after one of them – 'He (Anton Karas) only did that one song. He used to play at a restaurant in Vienna, you know. But people never went to eat there, they just used to come to see *him*, to hear him play.'

I keep looking at the clock hanging from one of the buildings, thinking, 'I've got to do an hour.'

The charity shop lady from last week appears –

'Can you come and play for us tomorrow? – You remember?'

'Oh yeah. How long do you want me to play for?'

'An hour? Two hours?'

What does she want – my blood?

When my time here's almost up, two young musicians – Guy and Helen, appear. They've got a clarinet, a mic stand and a brown suitcase. They've been playing outside Thomas Cook, but have been offered a couple of free tickets to travel somewhere else, as their drum is too loud! I tell them they can have this spot as I've had enough of the cold and my hands have seized up. I'll do just one more – The Third Man, of course. I start and Guy starts banging away on his suitcase in time. I endure this 'invasion' for one verse, and then stop.

'You're louder than I am!'

I don't need a beat keeper – I play fingerstyle, Merle Travis/Chet Atkins, the beat and the bass are all there, or they should be. Took me years to learn! I leave them to it.

Earnings: £2.26

DAY 34   **Saturday January 29th 2011**
             Winchester High Street, opposite WH Smiths
             Time: 2:55-5:25pm

Cold, cold – always cold! Nothing worth writing about for this session, apart from what I was doing before. Met Mr. Napier, the chief reporter from the *Hampshire Chronicle*. He likes some of the diary and it is arranged for some excerpts to appear in the next edition of the paper. Stuart, his photographer turned up, took some pictures opposite Smiths – I had to tell Rob, the rock busker, not to worry as I wasn't going to play, just set up my stuff for a photo – then Mr. Napier bought me a cup of coffee, had a chat, and that was it.

Next up was the charity shop refit do. Played just inside the door, on the left, for two hours and for nothing *and* I had to sit watching the owner's son munching on a hamburger while 'manning' the till – he was supposed to get one for me at the same time but he forgot, or he couldn't be bothered. I eventually got him to find his mother, get some money off her and go get one for me. Apart from that, nothing of note occurred …

apart from a man walking in wearing an old raincoat, Fedora and dark glasses – while I was playing The Third Man. Good timing.

Earnings: £17.81

DAY 35

**Monday January 31st 2011
Winchester High Street, opposite Clinton Cards
Time: 2:25-4:25pm**

Spent ten minutes deciding where I should set up – opposite Smiths or further down. Which place was warmer? Not much in it, so I go back to the usual place, opposite Smiths. I set my guitar and bag down, then hear a noise. I turn and see the small drum beggar, who I've had dealings with recently. He's sitting down in front of a shop; I didn't even know he was there.

'Go down the other end,' he barks.

'You're not busking,' I say.

He's not, as he's not a musician. He hasn't even got his little drum he hits in his random fashion. But wait, he's versatile and produces a harmonica from his coat pocket. He feebly blows into it and out comes one note. Not a tune. A note. However, in the eyes of the law, he is now a busker, and therefore entitled to stay where he is. It's me that has to move.

Remembering him shouting to me the other day, I say, 'By the way, I don't respond to people shouting at me from a distance.'

'I wasn't shouting,' he says.

'You were a few days ago.'

I leave and set up further down. Nothing to note, apart from playing The James Bond Theme several times in memory of John Barry who died yesterday.

A woman got off her bike and came over to give me some money. 'That's very fitting,' she remarked, as she acknowledged my touching, personal tribute.

Earnings: £15.72

DAY 36   **Wednesday February 2nd 2011**
                     Winchester High Street, next to Accessorize
                     Time: 12:30-3:30pm

Another new location, in front of a big old brown wooden door that looks like it hasn't been opened for many a year. I am hoping it remains in this state for my duration. I like this door. I feel secure in front of it. An almost mild day, and I am able to play pretty much non-stop. The money takes a long time to accumulate and works out at about £6.50 an hour.

About an hour in, a lady comes up.

'That's a nice guitar. You know, me and some friends are going up to Snowdon for a walking holiday with some guitars, what do you call them ... acoo, something, what are they?'

I help her out. 'Acoustic guitars?'

'Yes, acoustic guitars. People play them as we walk. It's a walking acoustic holiday, you know.'

A Walking Acoustic Holiday. I've never heard of one of them before but there's a first time for everything, they say.

Later, a middle-aged man comes up during The Third Man.

'That's a very nice guitar.' (My guitar must look more shiny than usual today.)

'Do you have a guitar?' I ask.

'Oh no, I don't play myself, but I have got some friends who play – Eric Clapton, Dave Gilmour. In fact I know them quite well, they're good friends of mine – see them all the time.'

What's this? – He knows famous guitar players? I think quick –

'Here's a copy of my album! It's had loads of good reviews! You can have it for nothing!'

'Oh no, you mustn't,' says the man.

'Oh yes, I must!' say I.

'And Bruce Dickinson,' he adds to his list.

'What, the orange guy? Dickinson's Real Deal, him?'

'No, you know, the singer. He's a singer.'

'Oh yes, he's very famous. He's in... what's the name of his group? I can't think... I know they play quite heavy, loud rock, don't they? And they've been around for a long time, haven't they? Who are they?'

This man can't remember either! He looks at my shoes.

'What make are those?'

'Samuel Windsor, two pairs – sixty quid. They're the most comfortable shoes ever, but they fall apart quickly.'

'What size are you?' he asks.

'Ten.'

'Oh. I've got this pair of shoes, size 9½ here.' He's got them in a bag. 'My sister bought them for me in 2002, and they're the wrong size. I've taken them up to Russell and Bromley, but they don't do that line any more. These have got a sort of frilly bit on, they won't have them back.'

I think about his predicament. 'You need to put them up on eBay. Do you have a computer?'

He doesn't and he doesn't know what eBay is, however his neighbour is a programmer and he's going to ask him to put the shoes up for auction.

About halfway through my session I am bombarded by clumps of soil and debris. It's the birds throwing it out of the guttering above. Yep, they're busy little buggers.

Earnings: £19.81

Note: The man with the famous friends came up to me a few days later, after the feature in the *Hampshire Chronicle* was published. He said he'd read it but didn't want me to ever write about *him*. I said I wouldn't, which is sort of true, as I haven't mentioned his name! Interesting, though – it seems people enjoy reading about other people but don't want other people to read about them. Not In My Back Yard.

DAY 37   **Friday February 4th 2011**
               Winchester High Street, opposite WH Smiths
               Time: 1:20-5:20pm

The Diary of a Winchester Busker feature came out yesterday in the *Hampshire Chronicle* – 'available from all good newsagents' – and I had a few people come up and say they liked it. A lady who works for a sister paper stopped and said that it was the last excerpt that made it for her, about the young man who never smiled. 'I felt terrible for him…' she said. There were also a few who said 'Great article!' as they walked by. Not all of them 'gave'. In fact, I was hoping for a bit more weight in the old hat today, due to the article, but on counting, it worked out to about £8 an hour – which is not too bad considering I stopped playing to talk more than usual today.

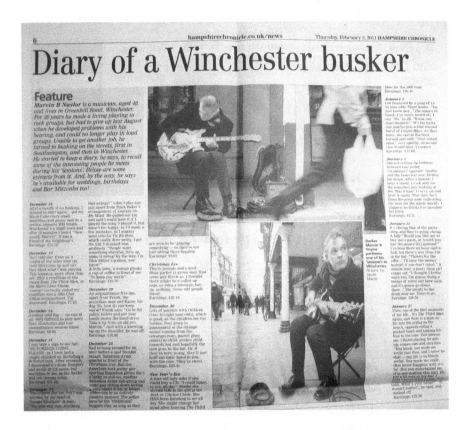

Other people seen/met today… Sue, a lady with such a quiet voice, I could barely make anything out. She does massage therapy but insists on seeing her clients at night as, if she sees them in the morning, they're useless for the rest of the day. Hmm, makes sense I suppose. Sue also does some mime, and is one of those you see standing very still, in a strange and uncomfortable position in the high street. To prove it she demonstrated by gradually slowing her head and arm movements until she was standing in a strange and uncomfortable position while looking at me. She remained like this for about thirty seconds, which seemed a lot longer and freaked me out a bit.

Also seen, two strange teenagers in matching plaid jackets. A boy and girl, both quite short. They started dancing in a hyperactive, super-quick way next to me, then went away and came back half an hour later and did it again. I've seen them many times before around this area. Very odd indeed.

A funny thing. Just after I set up, Mr. Napier, the chief reporter responsible for 'the article'* (apart from myself, of course) was walking by. He showed me what he had just bought – a DVD of The Third Man. 'I've had that tune in my head ever since I read about it in your diary.' So I *have* contributed something to the Anton Karas Estate, after all.

Earnings: £34.85

* How I'm going to refer to it from now on.

DAY 38 **Saturday February 5th 2011**
Winchester High Street, next to Accessorize
Time: 2:55-4:55pm

Some more people coming up to say they enjoyed 'the article.' Someone who likes it less than others is Rob, the American rock guitarist. I passed him when I came into town; he was busking at the top, opposite WH Smiths. After he finished for the day, he walked by me and said 'I saw your article, hey, I'm not American! Just 'cause I play American music, doesn't mean I'm American!' I reckon that kind of reaction can mean only one thing – he's Canadian. Canadians don't take kindly to being called American.

Frank the accordion player dropped by and mentioned the article – 'I didn't say "take a tip from an old *pro*," I said "take a tip from an old *timer!*" Anyway, you'll be more famous than me, now!' Frank's been in the local papers several times over the years, from protesting about whatnot to raising money for charity. He thinks I should get the article blown up double size and displayed next to me when I'm busking, but I'm afraid flagrant opportunism just isn't my style. I don't know, maybe that's why I've ended up here, busking.

After an hour and a half I feel I am getting on the nerves of the people working in the jewellery shop opposite my pitch, 'He's playing that bloody song (The Third Man) AGAIN!' Maybe I'm paranoid. The two women keep looking at me and not smiling. Or maybe they're bored. Some of these shops never seem to have any customers. Then a young man appears (manager?) and joins them in looking at me and not smiling. Then one goes away for a minute, and then there are two looking at me. Then one comes back, but doesn't look at me, so there are still two looking at me... then three... I suddenly remember enquiring about busking in Winchester. In Southampton I needed authorisation. I had to apply eight days before the day I wanted to busk and they had to send me a letter giving me permission to be at a certain place at a certain time. I also had to have authorisation to use 'limited amplification'. In Winchester you don't need a license but you are advised to limit the performance time to not more than one hour. It's an unwritten rule, apparently. I'm wondering if these people in the jewellers know this. In any event, they don't come out to me (which would have made their day more interesting, I feel), so I carry on.

Earnings: £20.79

Note: I found out later that Rob is English, from Portsmouth – nowhere near Canada… or America. No wonder he was annoyed.

DAY 39   **Tuesday February 8th 2011**
              Winchester High Street, opposite Clinton Cards
              Time: 1:05-4:35pm

Several people come up and say they like the article, none stay for very long, apart from the man who I met a few days ago (friend of E. Clapton, Bruce Dickinson) who stayed a bit longer, but only to say again that he didn't want me to write about *him!* So I (again) said I wouldn't! He asked me if I would like a cup of coffee. I said no thanks, I don't drink much coffee, especially when I'm out here – I need to keep playing. He goes away and watches me from the other side of the street for ten minutes. I have my head down for a while and when I look up, he's gone. But a few minutes later, he returns and hands me a cheese and lettuce sandwich and a bottle of apple juice he's bought from Greggs, nearby. That must have cost him £4 at least. I would have preferred the money! This brings to mind Frank telling me about the woman who regularly plonks a tin of dog food in his accordion box. His dog doesn't like it! I don't mean to appear ungrateful, but I'm a bit annoyed about this, so I *will* write about him.

Later on, after a Third Man rendition, I met a very nice old Italian lady named Delia. She told me about the time when she met Alida Valli – the lady who plays the 'romantic interest' in the film The Third Man. She met her during the interval in a performance at the opera house in Rome. 'She was very beautiful – she had a lovely profile! And she was very small, you know, like me (Delia's well under 5')… she was in another film as well – Piccolo Mondo Attico.' – I had to get her to spell it out for me. I told Delia about the story of Anton Karas having to re-record the entire zither soundtrack when the tape reel was destroyed in a fire. Delia is a very nice lady who must be eighty-five at least. She's been in England for sixty years and been married twice – both husbands dead.

Earnings: £38.75

DAY 40   Friday February 11th 2011
Winchester High Street, opposite WH Smiths
Time: 11:55-4:15pm

I couldn't busk for a few days, hence the long session today. I began the proceedings in the usual manner, with The Third Man, naturally. Every time I'm at this spot, there is a girl holding up an Asgard placard outside WH Smiths. I don't think she can hear me, as she's always wearing headphones/earmuffs. I never see her with anyone, but now there is a young guy talking to her and pointing at me. Maybe he's seen the article – he's coming over.

'That's from Spongebob Squarepants!'

'What? No, it's from a film…'

He interrupts me. 'No, it's from Spongebob Squarepants!'

'No, it's from an old film called The Third Man, but I think there was an arrangement in the Spongebob thing.'

'Are you sure?'

'Yep, it's from 1949.'

He walks away saying 'Play some slipper!'

'Sorry, what?'

'Play some SLIPPER!'

Or something like that. Anyway, he's gone. Good.

A man comes up. Last night he drank two bottles of gin with his friend. They are both businessmen and have just set up some internet company. This guy loves my playing and is promising to do great things for me. He isn't from Winchester, but is here visiting his 'aged mother and my children, who are younger than my grandchildren, you know what I mean?' He says he can get me 5 or 6 gigs in Bordeaux. I won't get paid, but it'll be a nice holiday. I can stay with him and his wife. I tell him about the article.

Delia from St. Cross

'Hampshire Chronicle? What's that? Listen, there are two ways of getting a million quid; one – you get someone to give you a million, two – you get a million people to each give you a pound...' He returns later with his aged mother. 'I've seen you before, I read your article.' She hasn't given me any money before, she does now.

Another woman says, 'I usually walk past you because you don't look homeless.' Later on, it's Delia with her trolley.

'Is this you?' She gets the newspaper out of her trolley all folded up right so you can see the article.

'Yes it is, Delia.'

'I didn't know if you had seen it. I thought you might like it!' (isn't Delia sweet, I think). I tell her how the article came about.

'Well, I was telling my son about the guitar player in the town and he went upstairs and came down with this...'

I say yes, I've been keeping a diary, and I tell her about the man who asked me not to write about him. I ask her if she minds me writing about her.

'Oh no, I'm old, I don't care what anyone thinks about me! Say it's Delia from St. Cross.' Delia was quite adamant I get the St. Cross in.

She gets a pound coin from her purse. I don't want it; she gave me some money the last time. She ignores me.

'I haven't much to give you, I'm on a pension. I can't do it every time!'

'I don't want it, Delia!'

She goes over the story of when she saw Alida Valli at the opera house, as I'm not sure of some of it. She likes telling this story. It's a good little story. I like Delia (from St. Cross); she's a very nice, lovely lady.

Earnings: £44.45

DAY 41

Saturday February 12th 2011
Winchester High Street, opposite Phase Eight
Time: 1:20-6:20pm

A busy day for shoppers – the busiest I've seen since I started busking and the most buskers I've ever seen in Winchester – I counted seven in the very small stretch that is the pedestrian precinct, none more than 30 feet from the next. So, from the top to the bottom of the high street, or in other words, from WH Smiths to Marks & Spencer: 1. Guy and

Helen, 2. Frank, 3. Glenn the conjurer, 4. Female violinist, 5. Young man on guitar and girl wearing much eye makeup, singing, 6. Two men – guitar/ukulele, 7. 18-piece steel drum band... and a guy singing and strumming a guitar next to The Slug and Lettuce pub in the market square just off the high street.

So, Frank was there, down a bit from the tweedle-dee folk muzak duo – Guy and Helen. They might as well have a couple of Morris dancers with them. I'm afraid Frank and I don't appreciate this music. It doesn't 'go anywhere', there are no dynamics, and why they need the music in front of them, I don't know. It just repeats ad infinitum... Then again, my Third Man tune doesn't go anywhere, either. Still, that'll teach young Guy to bang away on his suitcase during any more of my sessions. Frank says I can have his spot at 1 o'clock, so I am forced to amuse myself for an hour.

After going to the public toilets, I have a chat with Simon, the Big Issue-selling busker, who is sitting inside the arch where the flower seller is on weekdays. Simon seems a nice guy and I detect an unmistakable northern accent – Manchester I reckon. He often busks in the late evening, between 11 and 2am. It's a bit dodgy at times – he has to watch out for the drunks, staggering around and being aggressive. I then go to the cathedral grounds and eat my scone and drink my grape squash. I walk around the market square and see the guy (Rick Tarrant) outside The Slug and Lettuce strumming away, singing the popular Eagles dirge, Take It Easy... back to the high street, back again to the square, down the path next to the cathedral, coming out near the bottom of the high street. I lean against a column in the covered bit – The Pentice, right near Glenn the conjurer.

Glenn says he's had a bad day, he says hasn't done one 'table' the whole time he's been there. 'I've never known it like this. I usually do at least one table an hour.' I haven't met him before. I feel sorry for him – he's come all the way from Fareham.

At 1 o'clock I walk the few yards up to where Frank is. Money-wise, he has had a good day, he says, but now I'm ready to take over! ... unfortunately, I end up averaging just over £6 an hour – a bad day.

Earnings: £37.76

Rick Tarrant

DAY 42

Wednesday February 16th 2011
Winchester High Street
1. Corner of Marks & Spencer. Time: 11:45-2:15pm
2. Opposite Clinton Cards. Time: 2:33-5:15pm

A man comes up after The Theme From The Third Man and asks me if I have been on 'the big wheel'. I have to think about this for a few seconds before I realise that he's referring to the ferris wheel in Vienna, where the famous meeting between Harry Lime and Joseph Cotton's writer takes place in the film.

'Oh, in Vienna? No, I haven't.'

'I went on that with my wife. She's blind now, her brain's dead. I pay a hundred pounds a day. Cost me forty-two thousand pounds so far. Anyway, keep playing that tune mate!'

I keep playing that tune. Even the flower seller knows it by heart, which isn't difficult as it's only three notes. He's also whistling along to Music To Watch Girls By, making this a very noisy spot indeed. It's very noisy anyway, with six buses queuing up to go around the corner every fifteen minutes. I start to stop (?) playing when this happens.

After 2½ hours and only £11.97, I leave this spot to Frank, who has finished playing up the road. I think he's moving in on The Third Man – he's asking about a chord change.

I move on up the road and end up making a lot more here in a lot less time. Some more people mention the article – not many stop to talk apart from Ragtime Phillip, who has not seen me for awhile, but has very kindly photocopied the article for me. I also hear that there are a couple of letters from readers in this week's paper, so I'll buy a copy tonight. A lady says, 'Your guitar playing is as good as your journalism.' Oh dear, I hope it's better than that – perhaps I can't disguise my focal dystonia after all.

The lady who gave me the DVD of the man who died for twenty minutes appears –

'Have you watched it yet?'

'Sorry – no, I haven't yet, it's on the kitchen table. I'll watch it tonight, I promise.'

Earnings: £41.30

More Marvin B Naylor please

SIR — I enjoyed reading about the diary of a Winchester busker (*Hampshire Chronicle*, February 3), pictured above.

It gave us a snapshot of what happens on the High Street when the rest of us aren't there.

Please sign him up, I want to read about his adventures/experiences every week.

David Brown,
Upton Grey Close,
Harestock,
Winchester.

*Letter to the
Hampshire Chronicle,
February 10th 2011*

DAY 43

**Thursday February 17th 2011
Winchester High Street
1. Corner of Marks & Spencer. Time: 1:40-4:20pm
2. Opposite WH Smiths. Time: 4:45-5:47pm**

I'm down here at the noisy end of town again, because there are some young strummers at my usual spots up the road. Like yesterday, the whistling flower seller helps me with The Third Man, La Vie En Rose, Mr. Sandman, Music To Watch Girls By and many, many more...

A lady comes up whom I met about 6 years ago when I posed for a life drawing class at the adult learning centre – adorned with clothes, I might add... and 12-string guitar. I saw an ad in the paper – £10 for an hour's 'work', sitting on a small platform, occasionally playing, while a few people sketched me. Now, six years down the road they still need models and it's still £10 an hour... and it's *still* Val who's running it. I've now got her number and I'm going to ring up... soon. It's a guaranteed £10 and a damn sight warmer than sitting around here.

Later on, a very entertaining lady speaks to me. She moans about having to get a bus or a taxi to her home in Twyford since her doctor banned her from driving after she had two minor strokes.

'So I threw a brick through his window. I made sure there were no children about first, though.'

That was thoughtful, I said. Could she take to cycling perhaps? She thinks it's not a bad idea, but 'I don't know. I'm seventy-three, I don't want to be bumped off into a hedge.'

I can understand. I cycled a few times from Winchester to various places a few miles away and could not relax. There was always a car coming up at 70 miles an hour, or, if not a car, the sound of one from a distance. I timed it once – there was not a minute when there wasn't a car or truck, or the sound of one practically on top of me.

'…and these trucks go really fast,' I said.

'Well, some of my pupils used to stop and give me a lift, if they ever saw me. They were all very good drivers. A lot of them became truck drivers.'

'You used to hitch-hike?'

'Oh yes, and they all stopped – "You were the best teacher I ever had," they all used to say to me.'

'You were a teacher?'

'Oh yes, taught the rough, toughs and scruffs *and* I've had six books published and one was translated into Spanish!'

Her name was Mabel, ex-teacher, writer and a very entertaining character. I only realised afterwards that this was the very same lady who I met a few days ago and who, when I told her my age, said I looked a lot older.

After a long time here, I decide to pack up but can't decide if I should go home or do a short session opposite WH Smiths – if it's free, that is. I go to the toilets to wash and warm my hands up and then go to the cathedral grounds to count my fortune. I decide to do a short set… It turns out to be a good decision, as I make about £15 in an hour. Of course the minute I start to play, the pasty shop lady comes out to dump her bucket of sludge. I should know this by now – the daily ritual of the sludge-dumping…

Earnings: £41.47

An interesting observation made by Mabel: Men drivers are always much more kind and considerate than women drivers.

DAY 44   Friday February 18th 2011
Winchester High Street
1. Corner of Marks & Spencer. Time: 4:15-5:45pm
2. Opposite WH Smiths. Time: 6.00-6:25pm

I came in to do another late session opposite WH Smiths, as it proved quite profitable last night. Coming into the high street I passed two buskers I don't know – a saxophonist and a guitarist outside Barclays Bank – an uncommon spot. Down a bit, at the popular Winchester meeting-place that is the Buttercross, Frank is 'holed up' – to use an old Western movie expression. His hat is full of silver and gold, that's what we want, not 'shrapnel.' Further down, some lone strummers, so I'm back again at the noisy corner of Marks and Spencer. Ragtime Phillip drops by. The other day he was raving about a fingerstyle guitarist, someone Smith, who is on YouTube playing a Scott Joplin piece –Ragtime Dance.

'It's Richard Smith', he says.

'Yes, I watched him this morning, he's brilliant. There is also a video of when he was 11, onstage with Chet Atkins, he's great!'

Phillip has photocopied an arrangement of The Entertainer, which has the difficult C and D sections. I intend to incorporate these into my present C. Atkins arrangement. This will impress Frank – 'no one ever does those bits', he says.

A while later, and the excitement of the day reaches unsurmounted heights when I am approached by two police officers – a man and a woman, or more precisely, Police Community Support Officers, or PCSOs. I've seen them before, in fact I see the woman every time I'm out here. She says, 'I'm sorry, but we've had a complaint about you.'

Moi?

'… we're not asking you to move on, just to turn your volume down.'

I'm shocked. I'm probably the quietest busker of them all. In fact, I'm quite a shy busker. My (small) ego is bruised.

She carries on – 'Yes, someone in a shop up at the top –'

I interrupt, 'Today, you mean?'

'Yes, you were up there earlier, weren't you?'

'You mean up near Smiths?'

'Yes, near there.'

Wrong. 'No, I've just been here today.'

'Oh. Well, someone with amplification, we thought it was you. A shop owner complained they kept playing the same song – it was getting on people's nerves.'

Well, it couldn't have been The Third Man because it couldn't have been me!

Frank, who's been lurking nearby, listening, comes to my aid.

'Ah, I think you mean the two with the saxophone, earlier.'

'Yeah,' I say, 'Them! They were up near Barclays when I came in. I think they had an amp...'

I'm not going to take the rap for this! The cops must realise they've got the wrong man, but don't apologise.

I turn super nice and say 'But if you think I'm too loud, I'll turn down – I don't mind. I certainly don't want to offend anyone.'

'Oh no, it's fine, don't turn down, you're all right, we see you all the time, you don't annoy us.'

'OK. Good,' I say, '... and I see you all the time, and you don't annoy me.'

'Oh, OK, good,' says the woman PCSO. So, that's cleared up. Thrilling stuff.

A bit later, Jeremy and some friend come by and have a disagreement about the year of a Titian painting.

'Is it from the 1840s?' says Jeremy.

I tell them my favourite painter is Van Gogh, from a later period than Titian. Jeremy's friend says, 'It's amazing how many musicians say Van Gogh is their favourite artist. He's a real musicians' painter, it seems.'

'Really? That's very interesting,' I say.

It's getting dark and I'm going to pack up, or 'rig down', as the proper musicians say. There is a gang of teenagers on the bench opposite. One comes over and plonks a 2p coin in my hat. 'Sorry, it's all I've got, but your music is really soothing, we really like it.' A nice compliment, but I'm still going. So, off to the local WC to warm my hands, then up the high street. I can't decide whether to do a short session opposite WH Smiths or just go home. I walk past the shop, then back, then past it again, oh what the hell, why not! I set up and collect £2 within 5 minutes. Then, someone I haven't seen for ages – George, the 70-odd year-old, the guy who promised to get me some gigs – suddenly appears. I see him coming up to me, but he must think I don't recognise him.

'Marvin! It's me, George! Hey, I saw your feature in the *Chronicle*. It's great, isn't it! Have you got some gigs out of it? You must have.'

'No, not yet.'

'What? No? Well, it's great to see you – I haven't seen you for ages...' George then produces a £10 note and puts it in my hat!

'George, that's a lot of money, you don't have to give me that!'

'Don't say that, don't mention it, you deserve it, look – you're out here playing this great stuff... I've ordered those two Chet Atkins books, *Chet Atkins in Three Dimensions.*'

'They're great, George. The first volume's got La Vie En Rose – that's where I learnt it.'

George is in a very good mood and heaps a load of compliments on me. 'You'll be famous, Marvin (locally and fleetingly, I'm predicting)... bloody genius (untrue)... you're the only one here who plays Chet (true)...' George makes to leave, and I stop him –

'Are there any gigs, George, I really need some!'

'Not yet, the manager's gone away for a while, but I've got your number. I'll get you a gig, don't worry, and can I play bass with you?'

Oh dear, I didn't expect that.

'Oh, I don't know, George, I don't usually play this stuff with other people.'

George looks hurt. 'You don't want me to play bass, you mean?' He's looking even more hurt and now I feel really bad.

'Oh, that's OK, you can play bass George. Um, is it stand up or electric?'

'Electric,' he says.

'Sure, that's fine. You know all the songs, don't you?'

A few minutes later, George leaves – 'Phone me, George.'

Earnings: £29.48

DAY 45

Saturday February 19th 2011
Winchester High Street, next to Accessorize
Time: 4:55-6pm

A short, sharp session-ette at the end of the day. I am starting to almost favour these later ones when there are not as many people about. I seem to take the same amount of money, although there is no guarantee of anything in this game. My theory is that, not being caught up in the enormous wave of shoppers, some people may linger more and pay attention to the busker.

I'm at the same location as Day 38 – opposite the jewellers, and my impression on that day was that the three girls/women and boy manager were looking on me as an annoyance. Well, I have to say that their sinister behaviour today only confirms my suspicion. As they were shutting up at 5:30, boy manager comes to the front of the shop to shut the two narrow doors they keep open during the day. As he's closing one door, he says in a voice loud enough for me to hear '... it's really annoying,' while looking at me. Maybe I'm wrong/paranoid. It could be part of a conversation with one of the girls or could be directed at me, even though I've been there for only twenty-five minutes. However, I smile at him whenever he looks my way. I think – should I go over and ask if I'm bothering them? No, he can come over to me, or phone the police (or PCSOs, rather), which is what the shop owners seem to prefer – instead of just coming over and having a civilised talk to the buskers. They get the police to do the dirty work. Anyway, sod him; I've got guitar picks older than this guy!

Just before 6 o'clock, Ben, a friendly busker, comes by. I tell him my suspicions of the jewellers shop. Ben tells me about the time he was busking all day, every day outside the Laura Ashley shop, near where we are now. His girlfriend came by once and told him the shop had put a sign up in the window, just above his head, with an arrow pointing down. The sign, which of course Ben couldn't see, said DON'T GIVE THIS MAN ANY MONEY. He tells me he's been busking in Winchester for six years, which seems a lifetime to me.

Before they leave the shop, the people working in the jewellers must have to scan each other with a special jewel detector – I can see them all do this through the metal grill. Nothing like a company's trust for its employees!

Earnings: £19.53

Note: This is the first session where no one has come up and mentioned the article. Instant local celebrity can indeed be a fickle mistress.

DAY 46   **Monday February 21st 2011**
Winchester High Street, corner of Marks & Spencer
Time: 12:30-5:35pm

As often happens, I come into town intending to do a mere two hours and end up doing quite a bit more. The weather was overcast – it's never undercast – and it began to drizzle a number of times, making me decide to pack up, but then not bothering to. Today marks my debut of a new tune – not literally new in terms of being 'current' – none of my repertoire is, it's all ancient! – but a freshly learnt song – Tammy, the theme tune from the film called, strangely enough, Tammy, or Tammy and the Batchelor, from 1957 starring Debbie Reynolds – still alive, and Leslie 'don't call me Shirley' Nielson – recently (sadly) deceased. The song is sung over the opening titles by the Ames Brothers and later on by Debbie Reynolds at her bedroom window. I learnt it yesterday directly from a 1961 LP by Chet Atkins – Chet Atkins' Workshop. I played it on a 1959 HMV record player presented to Grandfather Pemberton by his employers upon his retirement in 1959 – pretty much contemporary with the album!

It was actually another song on the album I was listening to, as requested by George from Saturday, but this one appealed to me more. It has a real late 50s sound, complete with tremolo effect on the guitar. This is handy, as I have a little tremolo dial on my Roland Micro Cube battery powered amplification system… or amp. So I'm playing this song Tammy, and Jeremy appears, and he knows the song. This amazes me, as there can't be too many people walking around today who remember it. Jeremy says, 'Well, Marvin, that must have been meant to happen, as I'm probably the only person who knows this song.' Yes, it's gone down well. I play it again later, to Ragtime Phillip. He likes it so much he asks me if I will write out the tab.* Of course I will! … and I played it again later, for George, who indirectly directed me to it. However, Tammy is a tiring song to play, as it is all fretted high up the neck, and with the forefinger barred across all the strings. And my fingers are rather large for the narrow frets you get at the 'dusty end' of the guitar – 'stay away from the dusty end, there's no money up there!' as Chet Atkins once said.

Later on, a bunch of 14-year-olds walk by, one offers me a Dorito – No thanks. Another bunch of kids walk by dumping some shrapnel – 1 and 2p coins, heavy and worthless, in my hat. One of them accidentally spills something from a plastic cup, some sort of soup – carrot, lentil – it's yellowy anyway, on the ground in front of me.

Later… there are two PCSOs across the road – the woman I see every day, and a bearded male colleague. They are questioning a man on suspicion of walking with a mountain bike. They are talking to him for quite some time. The man – the detainee, attempts to escape several times but is restrained by the bearded one. I give them The Third Man as background music to their detaining.

* Tablature – guitar notation

It's very noisy today, with often six buses queuing up to go around the corner. After four hours it's getting on my nerves. I end up stopping whatever I'm playing when they are nearing the corner as no one can hear me anyway. I meet Alfie. I occasionally see him set up near WH Smiths. He's a pianist and busks with an electronic keyboard. He's not often out – I rarely see him this time of year. He's in his seventies and has a speech impediment and it looks like he's got some problem with his face. I think his speech problem must have something to do with that. I've heard him play the slow section of Chopin's Fantaisie-Impromptu, Opus 66 and that's not something you hear every day in the high street! So he gets my approval – and that's something not often 'got' in the high street, either. Alfie says he likes my Third Man. Actually, I don't know his name's Alfie until I ask him and then – because I can't understand him, I have to ask him again. 'It's Alfie, that's my grandfather over there –' he points down the road.

'Sorry, what?' I say.

'That's my grandfather, King Alfred – the statue (he laughs)… It's a joke!'

Earnings: £46.87

DAY 47   Tuesday February 22nd 2011
               Winchester High Street
               1. Corner of Marks & Spencer. Time: 5:15-6pm
               2. Opposite WH Smiths. Time: 6:05-6:35pm

A shorty in comparison to some of the recent marathons. I think I was playing La Vie En Rose – close behind The Third Man for most played song, when a lady in her 30s stopped to listen with her two toddlers – a boy and a girl. When I play The Third Man, many of the children like the 'wobbly' bits – made using the vibrato unit on my guitar, so I abruptly stop La Vie En Rose and go to the couple of bars before the wobbly bits, saying 'here's the wobbly bit' just before they happen. It turns out the lady is from Austria, married to an Englishman, and has actually seen the actual zither used by The Third Man Theme composer – the actual Anton Karas.

After a quick tear down of the 'rig', which takes no more than 1 minute – this makes me laugh, as when I used to play in rock groups it would take four people 45 minutes at the least to tear down or set up all the equipment. So, it takes 1 minute to rig down, 3 minutes to walk up the road to WH Smiths, 1 minute to set up – rig up? – and I'm playing 5 minutes after I left the first place.

At 6 o'clock it's quite dark, there aren't many people about, the pasty shop lady has been and gone with her sludge bucket. Nearby are two PCSOs – a man and a blonde woman, talking at the Buttercross, the well-known Winchester monument and meeting place for civilians and bored PCSOs. I've got my eye on them. They walk toward me. The woman comes up to me. Oh here we go, I think. But she's not coming to tell me off, merely to let me know that it *was* the saxophone duo that the complaint was about the other day. She's a nice police, no – WPCSO, no – PCSO...

Earnings: £10.12

DAY 48

**Wednesday February 23rd 2011
Winchester High Street, opposite WH Smiths
Time: 2:03-6:15pm**

A landmark day money-wise, as I was able to take home just over £50 for just over four hours playing. I normally don't get anywhere near this amount – the crowd are in a collectively generous mood today. Be more collectively generous – every day, I say! The weather was overcast and started to drizzle several times, but it wasn't too cold so I didn't have to warm my hands up, in fact I was able to play almost non-stop for the duration.

A man in his mid-forties comes up and studies my hand positions during The Third Man. I'm getting quite proficient at this tune by now, having played it 5,226 times before. We talk awhile and I keep thinking I've met him before. He is a guitarist himself, but unlike most guitarists who talk to me, this man is quite boastful of his talents – 'I've written a lot of songs (judging by his breath, he's been drinking a lot of gin, too)... some of them are great, I mean they're really great. I do all sorts of different tunings, as well. I tune down – I also tune up (I should hope so, too!)... Do you mind if I play a couple of songs on your guitar?' I tell him I'd rather he didn't, but he looks hurt, so, as I'm in a good mood – because of the weather, I let him play – but keep my amplifier switched off. He's the second person I have allowed to play my guitar today.

Earlier, a long-haired French teenager asked if he could have a go. I was in a good mood then, so I let him play his Purple Haze riff – with the amplifier switched ON, no less. But I find I look more kindly on the more youthful and innocent than on the middle-aged gin drinkers. After he finishes his songs, I ask if he has any recordings he can use to spread the word. He hasn't any recordings. He wants to keep it to himself, he says. But how will the world benefit – through all the up to date digital and internet technology – from his genius if the world can't hear it? Surely he owes it to all mankind. I get the impression he thinks it's too good and pure for us all. Oh dear... He tells me the story about a man named Alan Jones who played in The Shadows when he was 14. Said Cliff Richard was really only out for himself (really?) and didn't bother about anyone else. Well, I'm shocked – this goes against TV girl Fern Britton's gushing comments she made at the end of a recent TV interview with Sir Cliff, when she described being '... totally in the spell of this man and the Cliff effect... a wonderful man... makes you feel like the most important person in the world while you are with him...' Or words to that effect. Returning to Alan Jones, this man was playing with The Shadows at an outdoor concert in Europe, possibly Spain, when some guy rides on horseback to the side of the stage, dismounts, jumps on stage and sings a song with The Shadows. He was very good, apparently. Is there any film of this, I ask. No, there isn't. Was he a friend of Sir Cliff's – this young, bronzed, Spanish horseman? I'll probably never know.

It's when my man tells me he used to have long hair that I realise I have indeed met him before. It was a few years ago, in the pub around the corner. I remember it well. I walked in with my guitar case, he was sitting at the bar. I went up to order a drink and he immediately began telling me how great he was on the guitar. I asked if he had any CDs of his music. He didn't. Of course he didn't. I keep wondering how I should regard someone like him. I don't know if I should feel sorry, or not. They seem happy in their own world of no ambition, but who am I to say that's not the best way to be: no ambition – no disappointment. No unrealistic expectations – no disappointment. Hmm... maybe the way forward.

Later on, I've got my head down, concentrating on what I'm playing, then I sense a large dark mass moving toward me and forming an arc from one side to the other. I look up – it's a class of about thirty teenagers, aged 14-15, and all with dark hair. They are listening to me play The Third Man – performance #5227. They are completely silent, respectful and most have their hands folded in front of them. This has never happened before – a large group standing still, listening. I finish and they all clap. They are French students and are accompanied by two teachers or, to use an appropriately Gallic sounding word, chaperoned. Yes, they are very polite and I'm very impressed. Hmm... I wonder – would English schoolchildren behave in such a way? I think... *Non*. Many are then allowed to take photos with their phone cameras. I like them and say to the male teacher/chaperone that I hope they've had a nice visit to Winchester. He says something like 'It was fine, you know, apart from ze wea-thair.' 'Hmm – yes', I nod. Drawing on my vast knowledge of chanson – grand total of one, I ask him if he would like me to play La Vie En Rose as they leave. He knows it, of course, but his charges won't. I play a short version while he half sings/hums it. The children don't know it but are very polite. Yes, I'm impressed.

Earnings: £54.79

DAY 49

Thursday February 24th 2011
Winchester High Street
1. Corner of Marks & Spencer, Time: 1:40-2:40pm
2. Opposite WH Smiths, Time: 3:40-5:30pm

A remarkable day – in that there was nothing remarkable about it, apart from sandwiching a visit to the nearby surgery – an ear appointment with Nurse Claire at 3 o'clock – between two sessions. Therefore, I will take the opportunity to record for posterity – and my own amusement, a typical set list of songs I play for the good and sometimes generous people of this fair town. The list is in no special order apart from putting The Third Man Theme at the top. I believe this is only right. So, the song title followed by the composer(s), year of publication and, where known, the arranger(s).

1. The Theme From The Third Man (Anton Karas, 1949; arrangement: Chet Atkins 1960)
2. Mr. Sandman (Pat Ballard, 1954; arrangement: Chet Atkins 1954)
3. Chinatown, My Chinatown (William Jerome/Jean Schwartz, 1910, arrangement: Chet Atkins 1954)
4. Swedish Rhapsody (Hugo Emil Alfevin, 1903; arrangement: Chet Atkins, 1957)

5. The Entertainer (Scott Joplin, 1902; arrangement: Chet Atkins: A and B sections/Leo Wijnkamp: C and D sections)
6. Tammy (Livingston/Evans/Skinner, 1957; arrangement: Chet Atkins, 1961)
7. Yellow Bird (Keith/Bergman/Luboff, 1957; arrangements: Chet Atkins, 1962, 1967)
8. Music To Watch Girls By (Sid Ramin, 1967; arrangement: Chet Atkins, 1967)
9. La Vie En Rose (Edith Piaf/Louis Gugliemi, 1946; arrangement: Chet Atkins)
10. Ol' Man River (Oscar Hammerstein 11/Jerome Kern, 1927; arrangement: Chet Atkins)
11. Windy And Warm (John Loudermilk; arrangement: Chet Atkins 1961)
12. When You Wish Upon A Star (Ned Washington/Leigh Harline, 1940; arrangement: Chet Atkins, 1967, 1980)
13. Take 5 (Paul Desmond/Dave Brubeck, 1959; arrangement: Chet Atkins, 1970s)
14. Georgia On My Mind (Hoagy Carmichael, 1930; arrangement: Duck Baker)
15. Dance of the Goldenrod (Merle Travis, 1940s; arrangement, Merle Travis/Tommy Flint)
16. Farewell, My Bluebell (American Civil War song, 1860s; arrangement, Merle Travis/Tommy Flint)
17. My Old Kentucky Home (Trad. 1853; arrangement, Merle Travis/Tommy Flint)
18. Cannonball Rag (Merle Travis, late 1940s)
19. Solace – A Mexican Seranade (Scott Joplin, 1909; arrangement: Brett Duncan)
20. Lagrima (Fransisco Tarrega)
21. Estudio En Mi Minor (Fransisco Tarrega)
22. El Testamento De Amelia (Miguel Llobet Soles)
23. Choro De Saudade (Auguste Barrios)
24. Romance De España
25. Ave Maria (Bach/Gounod; arrangement: Alexander Gluklich)
26. Jesu, Joy of Man's Desiring (Johann Sebastian Bach; arrangement: Leo Kottke, 1969)
27. Angie (Davey Graham, 1965; arrangement: Bert Jansch, 1965)
28. The Theme From James Bond (Monty Norman, 1962; arrangement: John Barry, 1962)

29. As Time Goes By (Herman Hupfeld, 1931; arrangement: Marvin B Naylor – it's nothing to write home about)
30. Freight Train/What A Friend We Have In Jesus/Wilson Rag – Elizabeth Cotton medley; arrangement E. Cotton, late 1950s)
31. Theme from A Summer Place (Steiner; arrangement: Chet Atkins, 1961)

DAY 50   Monday February 28th 2011
Winchester High Street, opposite WH Smiths
Time: 11:50-1:10pm

Weather-wise, the past week had been mild, however it's all back to normal now. In other words, cold temperature, cold wind and breaks from playing every twenty minutes to warm my poor cold hands in my cold pockets. Just after I started, Alfie – the keyboard busker, comes up for a chat. Maybe we can get together and play, he says. He tells me there is a Pink Floyd 'tribute' group playing on Friday somewhere near the statue of his grandfather – King Alfred! I say to Alfie that I like the Syd Barrett era best. I notice he's wearing matching navy blue jacket and trousers – a suit even, attire I've never seen him in before. A bit later, a woman thinks I'm too good to be playing out here. I don't know about that. I'm definitely too cold to be playing out here, though. I know that!

'Can you not play in any other places?' she asks.

'I'm trying but I'm not very good at self promotion.'

It starts to rain and NO ONE feels generous in the rain, apart from the lady I met on my 'debut' in Southampton, so I rig down. When I leave, I walk past the bakery and see a man who gave me a pound earlier. He's sheltering from the rain and munching on a pasty.

'It's not often you hear The Third Man' he says, clearly not familiar with my reputation and/or repertoire.

'It's not often you hear me play anything else!' I say.

Earnings: £14.00

DAY 51   Tuesday March 1st 2011
                Winchester High Street
                1. Opposite Clinton Cards. Time: 1:00-2:35, 3:30-4:50pm
                2. Opposite WH Smiths. Time: 5:25-6:05pm

A long day, yet yielding scant profit – a mere £20. And like yesterday, a cold and windy day. Money was slow in coming and never increased in pace. A woman said that I brightened her day with MY music. Alas, it's not mine. The arrangements aren't even mine, apart from the bits on some records that I can't figure out. I have to improvise on these bits such as the 'tote that barge, lift that bale…' section of Chet Atkins' Ol' Man River. Even so, these precious compliments keep my spirits up. They *do* mean a lot! I played for over an hour but it got too cold so I rigged down and went to the nearby toilet and warmed – or rather boiled my hands under the tap – can't they ever get it right?! I count my change and have less than £7 for over an hour's playing. I go back to the same place and freeze some more.

A friendly Irish student, Josh, chats to me. He's doing a project about life in the street and would like to take some pictures of me. Of course he can. I'm sure there was a girl doing the very same thing last week. He gives me some change and snaps away. He gets a good one of an old lady giving me some money. I tell him about the article, rarely mentioned by my 'customers' these days. Right, I've had enough again. I pack up and am off to the toilet again. I eat my small apple and head off to the warmest place around – the HMV shop. I see a man struggling to read CD cover notes with a large rectangular magnifying glass. I approach him – 'Would you like me to help you find something?' He seems a bit annoyed with my offer of assistance but then says he's looking for Bruckner, as in Anton. We flag down an HMV shelf stacker/counterman. No, the HMV shop have no Bruckner. He's also looking for some Manhattan Transfer… Nope, they haven't got them either. Oh well, what they do have is warm air, which will do me.

I'm in there ages, getting warmed up. … I'm warmed up and bored. Hmm… let's have a look… no, they haven't got any Chet Atkins, also. What they *do* have, however, is one solitary CD of The Last Flight Of Billy Balloon. I remember going in for a meeting with the manager and persuading/begging him to stock this, about two years ago, and I'm sure this is the longest time they've had any CD on the shelves! They are always re-stocking them and I can only think my album has escaped some sort of deletion of old stock clearout. There's even a card with my name on it, which I must ask them not to chuck out.

I decide to do another session, this time opposite WH Smiths… After getting about £4, I'm getting really REALLY cold again. A man comes up – 'Do you remember me? I gave you my last pound, I was sitting on the bench over there', he points to the seat just next to Smiths. Then I realise that this is the same guy who came over and said I made him smile. I'm sure of it. This was the last excerpt from the article, the diary entry that a lot of people mentioned to me as the one they remember. I'm pretty sure, but not 100%, and I don't want to mention my diary business to this guy. I don't want to ask him if it was him who I wrote about!

Later, a woman would like me to play at the 'drinks bit' at a wedding in July, just around the corner in the cathedral grounds. She asks me how much I charge. I say £50. That's too much, so we agree on £40. Well, I don't agree with it but it's settled… .It's getting even colder now. I'm getting out of here.

Earnings: £20.01

DAY 52

Thursday March 3rd 2011
Winchester High Street, opposite WH Smiths
Time: 1:50-2:48pm

Like last Thursday, I came into town intending to sandwich a visit to Nurse Claire between two sessions, the surgery being nearby. However, it was so cold and windy that I aborted the second sitting and played for just under an hour for the grand total of… £3.35. Of the hundreds who walked by, only four gave generously. Even a minister – of the cloth, not cabinet, ignored me as he walked (very) briskly by. The kindness of Catholicism? Hmmph! If I'd been thinking quick enough I would have launched into What A Friend We Have In Jesus, but the cold had numbed my brain. The man who has a daughter who owns the place in Eastleigh where I played once, stops for a chat about guitars and amplifiers. Has he reminded his daughter that I would welcome another gig?

'Oh yes, and she said they all liked you. And you were cheap.'

Too cheap maybe.

After my visit to Nurse Claire, I walked back and forth up the high street several times, undecided on what to do; brave the cold and wind and risk getting only £3 or even less, for another hour's playing… or go home. I decided on the latter and vowed to never EVER forgive the people of Winchester.

Earnings: £3.35

DAY 53

Friday March 4th 2011
Winchester High Street
1. **Opposite Clinton Cards. Time: 12-12:30pm**
2. **Corner of Marks & Spencer, Time: 3:05-6:05pm**

Six hours is a long time to be busking (or doing anything!) out in the cold, even with a half-hour toilet/warming hands break. The feet take a lot longer to warm up – at least I don't have to play the guitar with them. I've noticed my right foot gets colder than the left. My theory: because my left foot is my tapping foot and therefore comes into contact with the cold pavement much less than the right. While on the subject of cold feet, my nice old Italian lady – Delia, paid me a visit. She says she is going to bring me a carpet next time she's in town, which are Tuesdays and Fridays. One of those small, square samples you get in carpet shops. Delia asks if I know any 'Roman' songs. Is this what Italians call Italian songs? I tell her I don't. She mentions a song she really likes called Dearly Beloved, from the 40s. I've never heard of it, but I promise to look it up when I get home. Surely Mr. Atkins covered it at some point in his long illustrious career. He must have done it on one of his 100 or so albums.

I try out a new number (I must find out why songs are called this) – Yellow Bird, the old Jamaican song of thwarted love. Harry Belafonte had a big hit with it. I've learnt a superb Chet Atkins (who else!) arrangement on which I keep making mistakes in the same bit – the middle break, or 'middle eight', where there is a combination of fretted and harmonic notes. I've practiced this a lot at home but keep messing it up. I apologise as a man gives me a coin – 'Sounds all right to me,' he says – the man with cloth ears.

A few people mention the article – I thought it had been forgotten, and one woman said the last excerpt – from Day 32, about the unhappy fellow, 'brought tears to my eyes' – Wow. Near the end of the second session, a man says 'Do you take requests?' Sure, if I know the, er, requested song. 'I wonder if you could play The Third Man song.'

Can I play The Third Man? 'I certainly can, I'll play it now! This is a 1960 arrangement by Chet Atkins...'

A bit later, another man comes up. He's just bought a banjo. If he brings it to me, can I make sure it's in tune?

'Are you here tomorrow?' he says.

I say I might be, I'm not sure, as it usually gets crowded with buskers very early on. I tell him I'm here most weekdays, though.

'Oh good – I don't want to make a date with you, don't misconstrue me!'

'Sorry? Oh no, of course not!' He seems friendly enough, although I notice he never looks me in the eye, not once. I give him my card and ask him to phone me to make sure I'm going to be in town so he doesn't have to carry his banjo around on the off chance he'll see me. 'I don't want to make a date with you' – what's all that about?!

Earnings: £40.53

DAY 54

Saturday March 5th 2011
Winchester High Street, opposite Whittard
Time: 3:55-6:30pm

As it was a Saturday, I came into town expecting to see loads of buskers but counted only two. Well, only one real busker, if you discount the small drum-hitting tramp, again displaying his musical versatility by blowing one note on the harmonica. He was at his favourite spot – *my* favourite spot, adopting his usual casual performance stance – half lying down/propped up against the wall. Down the other end of the street, a gaggle(?) of string/brass players, so I set up halfway down – opposite Whittard the chocolatiers, the shop that's next to Clinton Cards. I'm still struggling with the middle break of Yellow Bird but it's getting better, slowly. I'm trying to discipline myself into a format: To practice something till it's 95% there, by which time I'll have done it enough at home and will be becoming bored with it – to prevent that, it has to be brought out here – that'll sort out a couple more percents and the remaining 1 or 2% will never be achieved! I play Yellow Bird for about ten minutes, going back to the verses and break in any order.

The day turns out to be one of coincidences. During my elongated Yellow Bird, a woman comes up, plonks a coin in the hat and tells me she actually knew the man who wrote the song while she lived in Jamaica. Then, a bit later, a man (a regular hat contributor) walks by as I'm finishing The James Bond Theme and says 'That's really strange, I was thinking about that music about ten minutes ago in Sainsbury's and now you've just played it!' I agree – it is strange and it's not something I play a lot. Well, no more than once a day.

Other well wishers are two teenage boys who have a request – 'We were wondering, can you play your signature tune for us?' Unlike the man from a few days ago, these two are obviously familiar with my reputation/repertoire. I know what they want – The Third Man, and they get it, even though I played it five minutes ago!

Later… a man asks 'Can you play The Living Years by Mike and… what are they called?' 'The Mechanics.' I apologise for it not being part of my current concert programme. Anything else?

'Yes, Let It Be by Paul McCartney?'

'No, I'm sorry, I don't play any Beatles stuff.'

A woman with her budding musician son – 'He's been learning the piano.' I ask if he's learnt any Chopin yet.

'Oh no, but we've heard some great people – Alfred Brendel, he played the Broadwood piano at Hatchlands. He had all his fingers covered with plasters because of all the practicing… (I bet *he* hasn't got focal dystonia)… That was a few years ago when he had his seventieth birthday celebrations.'

I'm very interested in this. I remember when it was discovered, in 2007, that the Broadwood grand piano – part of the Cobbe Collection, was the very same piano played by Chopin in London in 1848 at a concert attended by a very young Queen Victoria. I ask the woman if, like me, she's a member of The Chopin Society – she says she isn't… and the way things are going, neither will I be – I can't afford to renew my membership at the end of the month.

Just before I pack up, a lady appears from behind me and hands me a book. It looks brand new. 'Here, you might want to read this – it's free, you read it and give it to someone else.' Which I suppose you could do with any book, but this one has a serial number at the back. What you do is, after you read the book, you go on a website, log in the number then give the book to someone else. That way, they can track the book's journey. I've read a bit of it already. It's called *Stuart – A Life Backwards*. It's about a down and out man. It's a biography but written backwards, so it starts when he's an adult and works in reverse to when he's a child.

I've read up to the bit about the so-called Cambridge Two – a man and a woman who ran a shelter for the homeless. They were jailed because, unknown to them, drug dealing was going on in the shelter, all on CCTV. They took the rap.

When I was packing up, I met an Irish poet – 'I'm a really good writer… my fodder was a very hard man – brought me up hard. I just buried him when my modder was killed by a car, outside da Coach and Horses – every bone in her body, broken…' To change the subject, I tell him about the article. He's seen it – 'How much you get fer dat?'

'Forty pounds.'

'Dat's shit money. I got four-hunderd an' fafty pounds jus' da odder day fer someting I wrote. You shouldn't be out here doin dis…'

Earnings: £29.91

DAY 55

Monday March 7th 2011
Winchester High Street
1. **Corner of Marks & Spencer. Time: 2:38-4:55pm**
2. **Opposite Clinton Cards. Time: 5:15-6:25pm**

The weather? Not too bad – temperature about 7°C or 44 Fahrenheit, hardly any wind. Didn't have to warm my hands in my pockets, not even once. First session proceeded without whistling – the flower seller has Mondays off. One of my regulars, a man in his 60s, pops up – 'I'm just on my way to the bank, I'll see you in a minute.' I play for an hour before he appears again. 'How are you today?' he says. I'm fine I say.

'Did you see my two wives?' he says.

I don't know what he means. 'Sorry?'

He seems put out. 'You know, those two women who were with me – my two girls.'

I try and think back to an hour ago and vaguely recall a couple of rather short ladies, quite young – early thirties, with him.

'Those two women with me, with the great big eyes – they're my wives.'

'Sorry?' I say.

'When I was working in Yemen – you remember I told you before? I was in Saddam Hussein's government for six years. Well, under Islamic law a man's allowed four wives – I've got two.'

I'm speechless. I've never met a man with more than one wife. I'm also curious – 'Well, um… how are *they*, you know – your wives, how are *they* about it, do they mind?'

'Oh no. The only thing is that, what I buy for one, I have to buy for the other – they have to be treated equally, so it can get expensive sometimes!' No wonder he was on the way to the bank. How does the British government regard his marital status, I wonder – and enquire. His answer – 'They only recognise one as being my wife, any others are mistresses.'

'Ah.'

He tells me he's writing a book about his time in Yemen. I say it should make an interesting read.

'Oh yes, it will – when I get round to finishing it.'

I'm at this spot too long, the noise from the buses is really beginning to get on my nerves, and more importantly – the money's not coming in. I'm starting to grunt, roll my eyes and tut loudly. It's time to move on! After a twenty minute toilet/warm hands up under the drier break, I move up the street and set up near Clinton Cards. A few minutes later, an idiot youth chucks three 2p coins, which land just outside my hat. He looks back and sees he has missed but instead of doing the polite thing and coming back, he sort of smirks and then laughs and carries on his way. I don't like to stop playing, but decide that if this sort of thing happens again, I will have to pick up whatever it is – always 1 or 2p coins, run after them and hand them back their rubbish shrapnel… which is what 1 and 2p coins are… unless you've got a million of them.

It's almost half past six and I've had a bad day. The sound of my own playing has become more than usually annoying and I've collected only £22 for almost four hours out here. Four hours! A little girl gives me a penny – at least she gets it in the hat so I don't have to run after her and throw it back at her! It's time to go home, but only after one last tune – Ennio Morricone's masterpiece – the mean, moody and magnificent Theme from The Good, the Bad and the Ugly. Steven and Holly recently requested I add a piece from this film – not the theme but another song from the film, but there's such a memorable and distinctive guitar line in the theme – everyone knows it and I just had to learn it! – last night in fact. I think it's appropriate. Although the street has no tumbleweed and I no cheroot, there is one thing I've got in abundance – reverb! I have both natural reverb – from the sound bouncing off the buildings on either side of a deserted street, and artificial reverb from the dial on my amp. I usually have it set to 4, but I now crank it up to 11 – 'How much more reverb can you get? The answer is – none more. None more reverb...' Yes, it's appropriate in many ways – I'm no GOOD for this lark, it's truly BAD it's come to this and I'm too old and UGLY for it all. Indeed. And with that, I say farewell to the darkening street of this one horse town... pardner...

Earnings: £22.33

DAY 56

Tuesday March 8th 2011
Winchester High Street
1. Opposite Whittard. Time: 12:38-2:50pm
2. Opposite WH Smiths. Time: 3:25-3:45pm
3. Corner of Marks & Spencer. Time: 4-4:45pm

A chaotic day spent zigzagging about, playing in three different locations. An almost mild day, the sun was out but people were keeping their money to themselves. A man stops in front of me – 'That's a nice guitar, you keep it in good shape don't you?'

'Yeah, I do. It's an Epiphone Casino. I polish it every day. I put the Bigsby on myself.'

'How long have you had it?'

'Oh, about six years.'

'I like people who look after their things.'

'Yeah, so do I.'

'Be quiet,' he suddenly says!

He doesn't say it aggressively and he doesn't raise his tone, he just says it out of the blue. It's bizarre! He then repeats – 'Yes, I like people who take care of their things. Oh well, goodbye,' and off he walks.

I say goodbye to a constant companion of these last few months – my large 1981 Charles and Diana Commemorative coin given to me by the Spaniard on Day 19, which I use to weigh down my hat at the start of my sessions. The French lady, who's always wearing the full length burgundy coat, was sitting on a bench opposite me. She came over, gave me some money and saw the coin in my hat. She really liked it – I told her it was almost worthless but she could have it if she wanted. I was quite surprised when she said, yes, she would like it. Oh well, I played La Vie En Rose as she left with my coin.

Later on, a lady I've met before – Mabel, gives me some money, looks at me and says 'You must be as old as me – I'm seventy-three.' Not this again. She said this the last time.

'I'm 48.'

'Really? Your hair's very grey, isn't it – mine's not grey at all.'

'No, and I know your name – you're Mabel, and I also know you've been banned from driving by your doctor and you've written six books and one of them has been translated into Spanish and you haven't got a bike.' She seems surprised I know all this and obviously can't remember meeting me and telling me before. Oh dear, it must be dementia. However, my music makes her feel cheerful, she says.

After more than two hours, I've not made much and decide to move on and walk down to the toilets near the corner of Marks and Spencer. Frank had put down his accordion and was taking a break. He was set up at the side of the bench in front of the shop. There was no one sitting on this bench at the time. I'd seen Frank earlier, as he'd walked past me, intending to set up at the Buttercross. However, Darren, who plays the didgeridoo – the didgeridoo guy I think I'll call him – was didgeridoo-ing. I said to Frank he could have my spot, as I was going to leave soon anyway. Frank fancied going back to the corner, but maybe later he might come back here. I said I'd visit him when I'd finished and let him know if the didgeridoo guy was still there. I had a chat with Frank, said hello to the flower seller, went to the toilet and came back.

'You've got competition today,' says the flower seller, nodding towards Frank who's started playing again. I look over and see the bench is now occupied. On the far side from Frank, who is playing right next to the bench, is a man playing a harmonica.

'I see Frank's got some accompaniment today. Is that other guy playing in the same key? – I can't hear him.'

'I think only *he* can hear himself, to be honest', says the flower seller. But there is one other person on the bench – an old man sitting in the middle, sandwiched between Frank on one side and this nutter with the harmonica on the other who's leaning right into him. It's pretty obvious that what has happened is the old man has sat down in the middle of the empty bench to have a quiet rest and take a load off his feet. Then Frank's started up and then this harmonica bloke has sat down and started blowing, or the other way around. Either way, they've both started within seconds of each other and this old guy's quiet, restful siesta has been transformed into a nightmare! He's wearing a flat cap and the most miserable expression I've ever seen. The flower seller says 'See that man there? When he sat down he had a smile on his face.' Ha Ha! Very funny – not for the poor old guy, though.

I make my way up to the WH Smiths pitch via the 'scenic' route – through the cathedral grounds, past The Slug and Lettuce – not the most scenic bit, stopping to read the prayer cards in the entrance to the small church at the end of the alleyway. Among the usual 'Pray for all the animals of the world', I saw this one – 'Dear Mr. God, I am tired of waiting here, condemned by the church. Please let me die.' I wonder what it means and if this sad person has ever walked by me in the high street...

I'm into my second session, opposite WH Smiths and it's Mabel again. She reaches into her purse.

'No Mabel, you've already given me something today!' I say.

She can't remember, but insists I allow her to give me a little bit more, as (once again) I make her cheerful. After twenty minutes Frank suddenly appears.

'Hi Frank, here – you can have this spot, I'll be gone in a minute.'

Frank plays, not right where I am, but where he always does, a few yards further up, at the Buttercross. I think he's had an altercation with someone in one of the shops, so doesn't play in front of it. However, the Buttercross is too near my spot, so two people can't play at the same time. I head back down the road to where Frank's just left. I get started sharpish, kicking off with The Theme from The Good, The Bad and The Ugly, to the delight of the flower seller. I'd played this earlier, during my second stint, and a woman walking by said 'Oh! That's my favourite!'

'Well, you've walked by at the right time.'

'It's great, can you play it again?'

'Sure, it's only twenty-five seconds long!'

Then, after tuning down – Yellow Bird. I've extended it as I've collected two £2 coins during the first minute... and it's Mabel again! And again she's opening her purse – she'll be broke, she'll get home and think she's been robbed, which she has been, in a way! I give up trying to dissuade her from giving me more. She can't remember seeing me half an hour ago, poor woman.

'Anyway, I like your music so much – I don't mind giving you some more.'

She's joined by a lady of similar age, who says 'Ooh, this brings back memories of when I went with my husband to Martinique.'

'Isn't it lovely!' says Mabel. Yes, Yellow Bird is proving very popular with the over 70s. Anything that triggers a memory goes down well.

Earnings: £29.10

DAY 57   **Wednesday March 9th 2011**
              Winchester High Street
              1. Opposite Whittard. Time: 12-1:15pm
              2. Opposite WH Smiths. Time: 1:25-3:30pm

Came into town at 11:30 but spent, or wasted rather, half an hour deciding where to set up. Had a chat with two young buskers – a guitarist and banjo(ist?) who were set up opposite the jewellers – a spot I avoid during the day as I'm not sure they like me… or maybe I'm paranoid… or suffering from a kind of persecution complex… The banjo man had a very authentic, what I would call a Three Musketeers moustache – curled up at the sides and augmented (nearby) with a goatee. They'd come from Andover and have been busking in Salisbury – 'We had a great time – didn't make much, though.' They haven't busked in Winchester before and it's not going well, money-wise. The guitar player is need of a low E string, which he has broken. He's in luck – I have one, a steel one, alas – however it'll do for his acoustic guitar. It's unusual to break a big, fat low E – the last one to break on me was, if memory serves, in the summer of 1983.

Where to set up camp… not at the top opposite WH Smiths, as there is a saxophonist/backing track/loudspeaker situation nearby at the Buttercross. Not down at Marks and Spencer – the 'noisy corner' – it's market day, and I'm a bit self-conscious about blasting out a few feet from the stalls. I decide to set up camp opposite Whittard and leave in disgust over an hour later with not even a fiver. I walk around a bit and have my snack of small sponge covered with chocolate and small apple and see what's happening at the top… I'm in luck – the saxophonist has gone and I'm a' goin' there! I've not been playing long when what's known as a 'real character' turns up to brighten all of our day. A man with a rugged, lived-in face, raggedly attired, mid-fifties I think but he could be ten years older or younger. He rolls up to me – 'Hey son, ye know Smooke On The Water do ye?' It's a Deep Purple-loving Scotsman. I remember the guitar riff which opens this song was so famous/infamous that at one point, long ago, it was banned from being played in some guitar shops. Later on, the same power crazed egomaniacs or 99.9% of those who 'work' in guitar shops – banned other famous riffs such as Van Halen's Jump and most Led Zeppelin ones from being played by budding young guitar players. I remember learning the Smoke On The Water riff – once learned never forgotten – and so, because I like this guy, he gets the riff, executed in the correct way – with the fingers – not a flatpick, to pluck the strings, just like how that strange, temperamental Mr. Blackmore used to do it.

My man loves it! He really does – 'WE ALL CAME DOWN TE MONTREUX… !' he belts out. He's bouncing around and playing an air guitar. This causes great mirth amongst the two workers in the shop across the pavement who were bored out of their minds a minute ago. I play the riff a few times, and then he says something unintelligible and rolls into the bakery behind me.

I play something else. He reappears – 'HEY! Wha' aboot SMOOKE ON THE WATER?!'

'Oh, I thought you'd gone.' I think I better play something else for him, but what? 'Do you like Led Zeppelin?'

'STAIRWAY TA HEAVEN?' he shouts without a pause. I start playing the intro. He goes nuts – completely nuts. He practically grabs an innocent man walking by – 'Jes' LESSEN te this guiy!'

Later on… an elderly couple walk past, the lady pops a coin in my hat then suddenly lurches towards me, saying aggressively 'I only like GOOD music!'

Later… another woman, in her 60s, stops for a chat –

'Do you know who you remind me of?' she asks.

'No, who?'

'Bert Weedon.'

'Oh… um, physically or musically?'

She doesn't answer this and starts talking about Eddie Calvert.

'I've heard the name, but I don't know any of his music, sorry,' I say.

She carries on – 'I like Radio Two, you know. David Jacobs.'

'Oh yes, he's been around ages,' I say.

'Hmm, yes, but I do wish he'd change his dentures – you can hear them when he speaks.'

As I'm packing up to go, my Ragtime chum Phillip turns up just in time for me to give him my photocopied guitar tablature of Mr. Sandman which he asked me to do the other day. He's grateful. It's no problem, I don't mind – he's a nice bloke. It's my good deed for the day – actually my second. My first was handing over my guitar string to the bloke earlier on – no charge.

Earnings: £25.10

DAY 58   **Thursday March 10th 2011**
Winchester High Street
1. Corner of Marks & Spencer. Time: 12:23-1:50pm;
**   3-4:45pm**
2. Opposite Clinton Cards. Time: 2:10-2:50pm

At the noisy corner again, with the whistling flowerman just across the way. As I start to play, he motions for me to turn up – I don't often get this from people! He comes over – 'You gonna play Ennio Morricone? That's great! People were smiling when you did that the other day.'

I say I will, but does he really want me to turn up? – I'm shy.

'Yeah, if I can hear my whistling louder than you, you're too quiet – crank it up!'

I turn up a bit. He goes back to his stall but comes back a minute later – 'Turn it up! Hey, do you know Here Comes The Sun by George Harrison – people'll like that one on a day like this' – it's half sunny, half not.

'Hmm, I don't know a solo instrumental version of it, although I used to play it in groups, you know, in a full band – I used to sing it!'

'Oh, don't do that!' he interrupts.

'No, I wouldn't dare! Um, I'll see what I can do.'

So, capo in the correct 7th fret position, I play through a couple of verses, the instrumental break and the end bit. It's got a good guitar bit that everyone knows so it sounds OK with just the one guitar. I could reel it off some other time while thinking of the next song to play. And someone gave me a pound so it's in! The flower seller likes a lot of what I play and he's friendly enough but I don't want to become tiresome so I decide to go somewhere else after my toilet/warm hands under the drier break. I move up the road, but I collect not even a pound in half an hour. I skulk back to the noisy corner. The flower seller is gone, replaced by a younger guy. 'THREE FOR A PAND, THREE FOR A PAAND!…' he shouts ad infinitum. Never anything else, it seems!

A man watches me for a while from across the pavement, and then comes over. He likes what I play.

'You know, all these people walking by – they don't realise the hours and days (and years – I already know what he's going to say)… and how you have to concentrate on playing this sort of music… I had a friend, in a band – we were both in it, he used to practice for hours every day, but he gave up, you know, with the fingers – he couldn't do it…'

I agree, it takes a long time to learn some techniques like the fingerstyle and classical way of playing. It's a lifelong vocation – and even that's not long enough, I say. I tell him about my focal dystonia – how I paid the price for my persistence and obsession. I'm blaming Chet Atkins. Actually, I found out recently that Merle Travis only used two fingers of his right hand so this gives me hope. Back to this other guy – he has an accent which I embarrassingly mistake as French – so I offer to play La Vie En Rose – he's Israeli!

Later on another man, one of my 'regulars' appears – 'Do you know any Greek songs?' – see the world go by at the corner of Marks And Spencer!

'Greek you say? No, I don't. Why Greek?'

'I'm half Greek, half Scottish. My name's Nicholas. My father was Greek and my mother was Scottish. I asked my mother what that makes me. She said "a mess only the gods can sort out"!'

Then my man with the banjo turns up – will I be here tomorrow to tune it up for him? Maybe, if it's not raining. A lady passing by during Yellow Bird – 'Is that Yellow Bird? – "high up in banana tree." My mother used to sing that to me when I was a child.' Instant coinage!

Earnings: £42.57

DAY 59

Friday March 11th 2011
Winchester High Street, corner of Marks & Spencer
Time: 1:45 – 5:50pm

Another long session at the 'noisy corner.' I used to avoid this spot, being quite exposed – and noisy, obviously – but now I'm growing quite literally attached to it. After a few minutes, the flower seller comes over and introduces himself and throws in a request to boot – 'Hi, I'm Bertie, you gonna give us Ennio Morricone today?'

'Hello, I'm Marvin, (and in answer to his request)... yes, definitely.'

The temperature's warming up a bit these days so I'm able to play pretty well non-stop. I don't even take my usual toilet/warm up hands under drier break.

A man approaches after a Mr. Sandman rendition, correctly identifying it as a Chet Atkins arrangement. He would like me to play it again. But of course! I try to do it a bit better this time – requests are special. Another man, about seventy, comes up after The Third Man and we have a talk about the tune's enduring appeal. I say 'It's amazing how many people know this tune – and of all ages, too. And it's mainly just three notes, right next to each other...' I play the three notes – da da da - da da – da da – '... and just three chords, too.'

'Yes' he says, 'and Dylan's songs are just the same – a lot of them are.'

We then talk about Bob Dylan and it turns out this man was at the Scottish university when they presented Bob Dylan with some sort of literary scholarship/degree a while back.

'He wasn't much of a showman – he just appeared, took his award and left – didn't say anything really.'

Bertie the flowerman walks past - he's taking a break – 'Just going to the pub – you don't think I stand here for ten hours without three or four pints, do you?'

Later on... a lady, early 60s, puts a coin in my hat, then – 'Do you know Jesus loves you? Let him into your heart and you'll go to heaven – you don't want to go to the other place, do you?'

I reckon it's too late, having played at most of the Working Men's Clubs in Devon, busked in Southampton and been to Dudley. I tell her I believe it is possible to be a good person without following *any* religion. She ignores me, naturally. I think about bringing up stuff like the probability of myriad alien life forms and how tiny our planet is but can't be bothered and she's got a glazed expression and it's a one-sided conversation with this lot... I would be wasting my (playing) time, although I could conduct a conversation *and* play something simple – The Third Man, at the same time but I'd still be wasting my breath.

'Yes,' she says, carrying on after my 'I can still be a good person without religion...' bit, '... but you will be PERFECT if you let Jesus into your heart! Do you know Billy Graham?' She hands me a leaflet.

'Yeah, I've heard of him – yeah, I'll read it.'

I gave up. I definitely can't be bothered going on about the Drake Equation – how there are X amount of galaxies containing X amount of life supporting planets – about seventy billion I think I read the other day... and the so-called Goldilocks zone...

'Read this and let Jesus into your life and start praying!' she says, still with the frightening, glazed look.

'OK!' I say. What I *want* to say is 'I'll take your money – you can keep your religion!' I watch her walk over to Bertie, poor chap – but wait; she's only buying some flowers. He's got off lightly!

Later... a man tries to get his toddler son to put a coin in my beret but the little guy just stares at me, open mouthed, and holds his arm out, five feet away. 'Go on (he says child's name which I've forgotten)... give it to the man, put it in his hat.' He keeps saying it, his son keeps five feet away, open mouthed, arm outstretched. It's taking us all more effort than it's worth. In the end, I stop playing, pick up my hat and go over, something I've never done before.

Another conversation about The Third Man – 'What is that actually called?' a man asks me. 'I think it's just called The Theme From The Third Man but there are other bits from the film that have proper names, like The Café Mozart Waltz, but I think this is just The Third Man Theme. Hm, I'll look into that – you've raised quite an interesting point there!'

I'm nearing the end of my session and I blast out The James Bond Theme just as Ragtime Phillip walks by. He's not heard me do this and is quite amused – 'Hey, I didn't know you were a rock star!' I think he's referring to my somewhat bombastic arrangement, which isn't very subtle, but faithful to the original, I like to think.

Earnings: £37.39

DAY 60   **Tuesday March 15th 2011**
Winchester High Street
1. Opposite WH Smiths. Time: 4:05-5pm
2. Corner of Marks & Spencer. Time: 5:10-6:40pm

I start the day's session with a selection of Chet Atkins arrangements – including The Third Man, of course. I'm playing to an old lady sitting on the bench across the pavement. She's soon joined by two other old ladies, then a third. This brings to mind the scene in Hitchcock's The Birds where more and more birds gather on the wire and then attack the terrified woman. I'm adjusting the scene and imagining these old ladies suddenly all coming over and pelting me with pound coins. At the end, as they are getting up to leave, one comes over, puts a coin in the hat and says 'I was the only one who guessed The Harry Lime Theme, you know!'

Later on… I'm playing Ol' Man River and hear a sound behind me – a sound I don't want to hear – the sound of a blues harp. It's the tramp who I saw last week sitting on the bench next to the innocent old man. The tramp sitting on one side, playing his harp, old man in middle and Frank playing his accordion next to him. Now he's inflicting the same thing – which I have to admit caused great amusement between me and the flower seller – on ME! What is this – some kind of poetic justice?! Well, I'm not having it! I turn and ask him not to play with me – he can go down the road and play there. He mumbles something and moves away. I start to play again. He's back and joins in. I've had enough and I don't care if he's playing in the right key – which he is – I've still had enough. I pack up and I'm almost done when he comes over and mumbles something else.

I lose my patience – 'Look, do I have a sign above my head saying GUITARIST NEEDS DRUNKEN HARP PLAYER?'

'Can I have a couple of quid?' he says.

'No.'

I leave for the corner down the road and keep looking behind to see if he's following me. I set up and have a relatively undisturbed hour and a half.

I meet Josh again, the Irish photography student who took some pictures recently, for his My Life – The Street project. He took some pictures of Bertie the flowerman, one of the PCSOs, the street cleaners, Big Issue people, the charity people… and me. He's been taking some more, but today he's asking people who are walking down the street if he can take their photo. Anyone. He says the businessmen – the 'suits', as they're known to us rebels (!) – are not very accommodating, to put it mildly, and an old guy on a bench wanted some money. He wasn't homeless or begging, he just wanted paying for it like he was a model or something! I say it's a shame how everyone's on the make now. Everyone wants something out of everything. I think of those old pictures from 100 years ago when people were thrilled to be in a photo in a street scene and they'd stop and pose for the camera – shopkeepers with aprons and brooms, people with bicycles, girls with big hoops! At least they're remembered in books. Yes, it's a real shame how jaded so many of us have become.

A youth who has been sitting nearby comes over. He's wearing a small 'pork pie' hat – all small hats are funny.

'Hey, you're not a bad player, d'you know any David Bowie?'

I know some songs of his, I know the chords to Space Oddity, but not for instrumental guitar, I tell him.

'How old are you?' he asks.

'Forty-eight.'

'You don't look too bad for your age,' he says.

I force a chuckle – he should talk to Mabel. She thinks I'm seventy-three. 'How old are you?' I ask.

'I'm eighteen – I've just had my first tattoo done.'

I think tattoos look stupid unless you're an ex-convict and/or work for the Post Office, or Popeye. They look particularly appalling on young women – and they all seem to have them now. It's been fashionable – in this country, no other, it seems – for them to get one of these horrible things done as soon as they get to the legal age.

Later on, a lady and her son listen to me. He's in his pushchair. They are Italian. He looks tired.

'He looks tired,' I say.

'Yes, he's been crying. We were at the park.'

'Oh, and he didn't want to leave?'

'No.'

'What's his name?'

'Philippo.'

'I like your jacket, Philippo – it's like mine, but smaller!' Philippo has scrambled out of his pushchair and has been given a 50p coin to put in my hat, but like other men(!) his age, he doesn't understand. He puts the 50p in but then takes out a pound coin and a 2p piece. Hey! I'm getting the raw end of the deal here! His mother eventually gets him to put the pound back and I say he can have the 2p coin, as a present.

I finish up with the theme from The Good, The Bad and The Ugly – with the reverb up, of course. A man comes from around the corner – 'I was wondering where that was coming from! I haven't got any money on me now, but I usually give you something – I've seen you a few times.' I say that's OK and I play it again – it works best at this time of day, when there's hardly anyone about.

Earnings: £21.30

DAY 61

Wednesday March 16th 2011
Winchester High Street, opposite WH Smiths
Time: 1:55-5:50pm

A cold and windy day, so it was back to normal or SNAFU, as they used to say in the war. Oh well, one must get on with it! I open the proceedings with a (despite the weather) somewhat chirpy rendition of La Vie En Rose. At the end, a friendly, suited man who had been listening nearby, comes forward to have a chat about musicians trying to be heard over loud customers in clubs, a possible small club venture he's thinking about and small businesses. In fact his business is actually called The Federation of Small Businesses. His name is Ward. Colin Ward – the Bond-ian use has relevance. After some minutes, Colin wishes to detain me no longer. We shake hands, he departs and I begin playing The Third Man. Then out of the corner of my eye I notice that Mr. Ward has stopped, turned slightly and is listening.

After a few seconds, he returns to me and says 'Why are you playing that?'

People usually say something like 'You were playing that when I walked up the street earlier!' or 'When are you NOT playing that?' so I'm slightly confused.

'What, The Theme From The Third Man?' I said.

He said again 'Yes, but why are you playing it?'

'I don't know – I play it a lot!'

Mr. Ward seemed quite dumbfounded, even shocked by my playing this tune. However he had good reason to be, because, as he then explained, it turns out he has just finished writing a piece about an actor whose first credited role was in the film The Third Man. And what's more, the man came to be in the film as a direct result of his association with Colin Ward's father! None of this I would have known had I not decided to play the celebrated theme there and then thus unwittingly turning a pleasant, everyday meeting into an extraordinary encounter. I mean, to meet a man who knew an actor in the film is one thing but to not know this and to start playing the Theme as the man is walking away *and* to find out he has just written about it, well no wonder Colin was freaked out. Once again, I am amazed at the connections made through this particular piece of music. Colin said he would send me the piece he had just finished and, sure enough he did, a few hours later. It told the story of how in 1938 Colin's family had taken in a family of Jewish refugees from Vienna, one of whom was Erich Pollak, an actor who appeared as the barman in The Third Man under his stage name of Erich Pohlmann. He had got the part in the film after Colin's dad introduced him to Carol Reed, who lived nearby. Erich Pohlmann died in 1979. Colin still visits Erich's sister Herta in London. She is 93.

Earnings: £26.20

DAY 62   **Thursday March 17th 2011**
Winchester High Street
1. Next to Accessorize. Time: 2:18-3:45pm
2. Corner of Marks & Spencer. Time: 4:05-6:20pm

Frank, his accordion, and dog Kazoo were down at the noisy corner and a young strummer halfway down The Pentice – the covered bit, so I've got no choice but to set up opposite the jewellers, about whom I am slightly paranoid – I don't think they like me. It was OK, I made about £14 in the one and a half hours I was there – not bad for me. *And* it was a mild day so I could and did play non-stop. Frank walks past, saying he hasn't had a good day and is heading up to the Buttercross – the famous Winchester meeting-up, breaking-up landmark, as the young strummer has gone. I fancy a change of scenery so head down to where Frank's just been.

Today seems to be the day when people want to give me things. One of my regulars, Gary, insists I have a banana from the bunch he's just bought. I saved this for near the end. Then one of a group/gang of teenagers hands me a small chocolate doughnut. This was devoured instantly. And near the session's end an Irishman, naturally named Mick, with a small Irish flag painted on his cheek, hands me a can of Guinness – a can of *draught* Guinness, too! He gives me another one a few minutes after the first – not because I've drunk the first one – never out here. He sits on the bench nearby for ten minutes between the two. And that's not all. Earlier on, a woman gives me a £5 note after my Leo Kottke arrangement of Bach's Jesu, Joy of Man's Desiring. 'Would you like some change, I have change you know?' No, she doesn't. 'Well, I thank you very much.' Also, after this tune, a man says my guitar sound is like a classical guitar. I disagree most vociferously with his statement, then we have a conversation about Spanish/classical guitars and I want to know why, oh WHY do none of them ever have any fret markers on the fretboard? None of them do. No fret markers on a fretboard makes me panic. I hold up my Epiphone Casino and show him its parallelogram fret markers. 'See, I know where I am with these – 3rd fret, 5th fret, 12th… with a classical guitar it's just a long blank space – I panic!' Hm, yes, that's my only complaint I have with Gretsch guitars, apart from the exorbitant price – most of them have no fret markers.

Just before I finish, two American musicians come by.

'Hey, d'ya play in a group?'

I give them my hard luck story – ears can't handle it anymore…

'Ya get any work in clubs around here? – yer good enough to play in clubs.'

I say I don't, but I've given my demo CD to the guy at Green's Wine Bar up the road, and even the dreaded Conservative Club, where NO ONE can hear you scream.

'Hey, just go in with yer guitar, tell 'em you don't want much – just tell 'em you'll play a few toons, maybe just get a couple o' beers from 'em, maybe they can give ya twenty quid, maybe if they like ya they can give ya more next time.'

I say, yes, that's how it should be – just walk in, etc. but I can guarantee if I go up to Green's and adopt that attitude, they'll run me outa town like a common pygmy!

Earnings: £37.73

DAY 63

Saturday March 19th 2011
Winchester High Street
1. Corner of Marks & Spencer. Time: 2:15-3:15pm
2. Opposite Clinton Cards. Time: 3:30-6:25pm

Arrived in town at 1 o'clock but couldn't get a pitch until over an hour later. Talked to Frank down at the noisy corner, waved to Bertie the flowerman across the way. In half an hour Frank says I can have his spot for an hour, so I walk up and down the street… talk to Rob who I insulted in the article by saying he was American! He was waiting at the famous gathering spot – the Buttercross – for Bob Jackson's rockabilly trio to finish so he could take over. Rob made an interesting observation – whenever he busked with a bass player they always got more money when they were playing a stand-up bass than when they had an electric bass. It certainly looks more impressive, I agree. Rob sings the praises of in-ear monitors when I mention I've had to give up playing in groups due to the loud volume. Maybe I should have had some years ago – I could still be playing in those so-called 'tribute' groups now and I suppose I could have carried on for another five or ten… or even fifteen (!) years, in complete anonymity – known only as someone who dresses up as someone else. Thinking about it, I don't think I could do it anymore. At least with the busking, I'm pretty much my own boss. I turn up when I want. I pick the songs I want to play. I play them when I want and in whatever order and play however long I want. And being solo, I haven't got to put up with egotistical and impossible to get along with musicians… and they don't have to put up with me!

My allotted time arrives and I do exactly one hour. The pitch's proprietor – Frank, the man himself, listens to my final few minutes from the bench opposite. He comes over to say he hasn't ever heard any arrangement similar to my, or rather Leo Kottke's, Jesu, Joy of Man's Desiring. Frank appears quite knowledgeable about music – or he thinks he is, and has mentioned a couple of times that his mother used to play Chopin, so I take his remark as a compliment. Actually, this arrangement has been getting a bit of notice recently and is proving a popular part of my repertoire, my thanks again to The Great Kottke.

Later on, up the road as I'm bringing my act (ha!) to a close, a couple in their 40s suddenly appear in front of me dancing what a man standing near me identifies as the Tango – the South American dance born in the lower class areas of Buenos Aires and Montevideo… Yes, dancing the Tango – to La Vie En Rose. They seem comfortable with the rhythm I'm providing so I extend the tune by a couple more verses – somewhat deftly, I like to think. The Tangoists (?) still appear to be having a good time so I again rather deftly start into The Theme From The Third Man – retaining an identical rhythm and extending it, like the first song, by a couple more verses…

After a few more minutes, I'm beginning to wonder how long this is going to go on for, when the male dancer says 'Can you stop now – we're bursting!'

Ha! Ha! Isn't it funny how polite we all are, I think. Me – to stop playing, and them – to stop dancing.

Earnings: £35.01

DAY 64   Monday March 21st 2011
                    Winchester High Street, corner of Marks & Spencer
                    Time: 2:15-4:25pm

On Monday mornings I haul my sack of gold – the earnings from the previous week's busking – to the bank on the high street and sometimes wander down the road to see if there's anyone in any of the busking spots. Today, I met someone I didn't know – Nathan, a five foot short 83-year-old busker wearing a flat cap, just setting up his hurdy gurdy down at the noisy corner. I was attempting to engage him in a friendly conversation – 'Do you come here often?' etc... but he seemed a bit wary of me until I told him that I too am a busker. Perhaps he thought I was some posh Winchester person as I was wearing my Burberry trench coat, second hand at least – it's more than thirty years old, I'm sure! But after that – when I said 'busker', Nathan relaxed a bit –

'I remember when Gypsies (he's one, he says)... and buskers were looked down on and sometimes even spat on. Now, everyone wants to be a busker.'

Well, I wouldn't go that far, Nathan.

He also tells me he's just written a book, called *From Rags To Riches By A Rascal*, or 'Rawcal' as Nathan's S's don't come out well. Nathan's definitely a rascal – he's got a low growl of a voice every rascal should have. He relates some events of his eventful life, such as being given the Freedom of the city of London and raising £230,000 for a Great Ormond Street charity. That's a lot of money for a busker to raise, so I repeated the amount, slowly enunciating the words so to be quite sure he heard. But it must be true – twice he confirmed the amount. He is going to do four hours here and asks me how much I make in an hour. I tell him if I can get £10, I'm content. He says he'll finish at 2:30 – Chinese dentist, so I'm going to come back just after two and hear his reconditioned 1922 hurdy gurdy device for a bit, then take over the spot after he leaves...

Later... it's ten minutes past two and I have arrived at the corner of Marks and Spencer and Nathan is nowhere to be seen. Oh well, I set up and start my session. About fifteen minutes in, Nathan appears from around the corner. Apparently he packed up early as he made only £11 for playing – or to be more precise, turning a crank – over three hours.

'I need more old people – who know what I'm playing. These songs – all these young kids don't know 'em.'

A fair point. I told him that most of my 'customers' are the over 60s. In fact, I reckon at least 80% of my money is from them. I felt sorry for

Nathan and was glad I bunged him a £2 coin earlier – I wonder if the £11 included that! Oh dear – eleven pounds in just under four hours – that's bad and I know how he feels.

Later on, halfway through my spot – I'm playing Ol' Man River and a busker I had passed on the way down walks by and stops a few yards away. He turns around and comes to me –

'You're quite good, are you a professional musician?'

'Thanks, well I used to …' I give him my hard luck story. His name is Colin and he has a couple of tips to give me, if I don't mind.

'First, you need to get a music stand.' He points to my blue plastic binder on the pavement. I keep this on the ground as it is in a direct line of vision just beyond my fretboard. I only need it for a couple of tunes I haven't got memorised yet, but I really need it to be there. Actually, Colin has a music stand. He also has several other musicians playing with him – they're very good – I've never heard them make a mistake. This is possibly because they are backing tracks. So the music stand can't be for them – it must be for Colin, who plays single note lines on his saxophone.

His second tip was 'Don't play more than two or three days a week – you'll get more money if you play less.'

Colin is wrong. I've played 2 days a week, 3 days a week, 4, 5, 6 days a week and I've even played Eight Days A Week. And the money's always the same. Colin says he brings in maybe £30 an hour. I don't believe him. But thanks for the tips anyway, Colin – and good luck to you!

Earnings: £18.16

DAY 65   Tuesday March 22nd 2011
                    Winchester High Street
                    1. Corner of Marks & Spencer. Time: 1:21-3:43pm,
                       5:15-6:05pm
                    2. Opposite WH Smiths. Time: 4:20-5:10pm

Had a pre-performance chat with Bertie the flowerman. He now greets me with 'Hey, guitar man!' then does the Third Man tune – 'do do do do do…'

Says Bertie – 'I had Frank here earlier. I was quite impressed – he did Brain Damage.'

Marcus and Jan

I knew the song title but couldn't place it.

'You know, Pink Floyd. From Dark Side of the Moon.'

'Oh yeah – the lunatic is–'

'– on the grass,' Bertie finishes the line.

Yes, now I remember it. All added up, I must have spent weeks listening to that album when I was 13.

'Wow, that *is* impressive – I'd like to hear that.'

I would – I must request it when I see Frank play next.

I look up during my session and see Delia from St. Cross across the pavement, waving to me. She is wearing her woollen hat and has her shopping trolley – the type all ladies over seventy have.

I premier a freshly learnt tune – Deve Ser Amor (It Had To Be Love) by the Brazilian composer Roberto Baden-Powell. It's a Samba, and my first – and possibly last – attempt at this musical form. However it goes down well – the money pouring in – all £1.75. After more than two hours I decide to move up the road but after half an hour I've only got £2 and am about to give up and return to the noisy corner when one of my regulars, Marcus, turns up with his sister or wife or cousin or something or other. She's one of these – hopefully she's just one!… but I can't remember which. Marcus asks me if I do anything else. I say I also do my own music, mainly using the 12-string guitar. I give him my 'original music hard luck story' which is a bit of airplay, some (mostly) really great reviews. But it doesn't pay. I inform him there is a copy of my album down at the HMV shop, available for £7. Then I remember I have a copy in the bag I carry my amplifier and camping stool in. 'Here it is, see!'

Then something incredible happens – Marcus wants to buy it from me – and for £7.

'Have you got change for a tenner?'

I sure do. I'm pleased he didn't go and buy it from the shop – they might not re-stock the shelf and the bit of card with my name on will be chucked away. Like I remember thinking before – I'm sure my album has been there longer than any other CD!

A suited man comes up. He wants to know if I can play at the drinks bit at his sister's wedding in the summer. Good, I need some more of these. I return to the first spot for a short, end of the day session. Just before I finish, the charity shop manager comes up to me – the same one who got me to play for two hours for her reopening awhile back, for no fee and a burger I practically had to beg for.

'How are you today, how's it going?' she says, looking down at my hat.

'OK today, the weather's fine, although my hands are starting to go a bit.' Even though the temperature is definitely warming up, after four hours outside, my hands are slowly chilling.

'Oh well, you ARE our favourite busker, you know!'

That's very nice of her to say so, but try coughing up some change now and again, love.

Earnings: £44.14

DAY 66   **Wednesday March 23rd 2011**
Winchester High Street
1. Opposite Vodafone. Time: 11:38-2pm
2. Opposite Marks & Spencer. Time: 2:38-4:10pm

It's Wednesday – Market Day. There's a lady fiddling with her violin – a fiddler? – opposite Marks and Spencer and a guy sitting on a bench halfway up the high street blasting out La Bumba or La Bamba or whatever it's called. He's got an amplifier like mine but I wouldn't dare play it that loud. I set up right near the spot opposite the jewellers but just to the side so they can't see me out of their window – I'm really paranoid about them! Ten seconds after I start up La Vie En Rose, a nice old lady – Daphne, stops for a ten minute chat. Her husband, now dead, used to be a singer but he never pushed himself. They knew one of the songwriters who wrote A Nightingale Sang in Berkeley Square who was promoted to a high position at the BBC.

'When he got the job, I urged my husband to send him a card congratulating him but he wouldn't, so I sent it myself – put his name on it. He wrote a nice letter back but my husband could have got a lot further.'

'Oh well, you must have some good memories of him. Did he manage to get on any records?'

'No, but he sang with some big names – some big bandleaders.'

'Oh well (I say again), you've got some good memories – that's enough isn't it.'

'Well, no… not really!' she laughs.

A man with the most wrinkled face I've ever seen comes up for the longest chat I've ever had. He used to be in the army in the '60s and went to Germany.

'I used to like all the cowboy gear, you know. I had a big Stetson hat and when I was over there I bought these trousers with the big flared bottoms and a holster to put my two forty-fives in. When I came back here I remember going to a pub and after a few drinks my mate said he really liked my gear.' (He went to the pub dressed like that?!) 'I said "Tell you what, next time I'm away I'll bring you something back," and so I did. Next time I went to Mexico I bought him back one of those wide brimmed hats – a Sombrero…' … about 15 minutes later… 'and I have a grandson. He got hold of one of my guns once and he cocked it, you know. Do you follow me? – you're not following me, are you?'

Not really, my mind was starting to wander. I needed to start playing again – I'll have to put a sign up saying NO CONVERSATIONS TO LAST MORE THAN 5 (FIVE) MINUTES PLEASE.

'Sorry, he cocked the gun?' I say.

'Yes, you know – pulled the little lever back – cocked it, then he fired it.'

'What?'

'It wasn't loaded, but I gave him a talk about guns and ammunition, though.'

'How old is he now?' I asked.

'He's twenty-five.'

'And is he in the army?'

'Oh yes.'

I thought he might be.

He went on – 'I said to him "If you can achieve what I have achieved in my life…" I was in Northern Ireland from sixty-nine to seventy-seven. Then I was a WO.'

What's that?

'WO? Warrant Officer – that's above…' he explained the relative ranking of every post in the British Army, then said again '… yes, I said to him (the grandchild) "If you can achieve what I have…" '

After an hour, I haven't made much. I've listened to much but not made much. There are a lot of people about and I'm hoping no one else stops for a conversation of marathon length. What's this – a lady is approaching, she's smiling at me and has something in her hand. I want it to be a £2 coin. It's not, it's a bit of wrapper or something, she puts it in the bin next to me.

Later on… a woman vicar stops for a *short* chat, thank God(?)! She used to play the classical guitar.

'Do you not play now?' I ask her.

'No, because I've got no end to this finger.'

Does she mean her finger is really long, I think. No, she shows it to me and it has no end – it's been cut off.

'And it's quite tender – it hurts if I put pressure on it so I can't really play.'

I feel a certain kinship with people who have problems with their hands and relate to her my particular problematic condition of focal dystonia.

I take a lunch break where I have my cheese and lettuce sandwich, chocolate bar and small apple in the cathedral grounds, which is full of other lunching people – it's warming up now. I count my money – only £9 for more than two hours playing – actually more like one hour playing, one hour listening to the above. I decide to set up camp where the lady fiddler was, opposite the corner of Marks and Spencer, which is where I usually play. The market stalls are too near the shop, so that's why the buskers are over on the other side.

An old couple on the way to the optician.

She: 'It's a pleasure to see such nice music here for once.'

He: 'Hear – to HEAR nice music, you mean.'

Another man – in his seventies: 'Do you do requests?'

'Oh yeah – if I know the song, definitely.'

'Oh good, you know there's a guitarist who sometimes plays up the road, usually on the bench and he never does requests – he's very good, mind – brilliant, but just doesn't do requests.'

'Strange,' I say.

'Yes, I think – what's he doing out here – but he's brilliant. And I like dancing and the other night I was out and the dance floor was empty so I went up to the band member and said "Why don't you play something we can dance to?" and said "Look at the floor, it's empty." Anyway, do you know any Spanish music?'

'Hmm, only a few things like Lagrima and my little Spanish medley.' I suddenly remembered my new piece – Deve Ser Amor, the Samba.

'I know a Brazilian tune – my only one.'

I play it – he loves it – I'm pleased. It's quite taxing for the right hand, especially for me with my useless fingers and it has a fast rhythm which doesn't let up. However, it's been going down well enough for me to make it Song of the Week.

This spot, which falls well into the noisy corner zone is very noisy indeed today. I've got the young 'THREE FOR A PAAND!' flower guy in one ear and the fruit and veg man shouting 'COME ON, THEY'RE GOING CHEAP!' in the other. Plus the buses… and me. Money-wise it's a bad day – £20 in four hours and I'm quite depressed, walking home. At the other end of the street I see Marcus – one of my regulars – the guy who bought my album from me yesterday. He calls to me from the other side of the street. He's talking to Alan, the guy who cleans the street who I see every time I'm out here, although I only find out his name now.

'I like your album, especially the first two, and the last song – about Francesca. Is that your daughter?'

'No, it's someone I knew a long time ago – she died when she was seventeen. She had something wrong with her heart. It got too big for the space where it was, I think.'

'Yeah, your album. I like it very much. A bit like a young Donovan, before he got famous.'

'I'm glad you like it – I was going to give you your money back if you didn't!'

Earnings: £20.97

DAY 67   **Thursday March 24th 2011**
Winchester High Street
1. Corner of Marks & Spencer. Time: 2:20-3:45pm
2. Opposite WH Smiths. Time: 3:50-5:42pm

The weather was fine today, though not much else was. I played for an hour and a half and took only £3.70 and I'm immediately transported back to October last year when I started busking in Southampton – the money was so bad – mainly 1p, 2p coins – I was barely making my train fare back some days. I'd really hit rock bottom. It's days like this when it gets the most depressing. My mind wanders. I'm embarrassed to be here – ignored by pretty much everyone – thousands. And I'm angry that somewhere down the line something has gone seriously wrong for me to end up here – that I haven't advanced or pushed myself in the right way and the end result of forty-eight years is sitting on a street corner playing for some pennies. I leave in disgust. I'm angry at the people for ignoring me, but I'm more angry with myself.

I move up the road – maybe it's better somewhere else.

Near the end of the session I notice a young man – about twenty, sitting on the bench opposite me. He's wearing a black track suit, has short, light coloured hair and is smoking. He leans forward with his elbows on his legs and is looking at me in a hostile way, which makes me nervous so I keep my head down. I look back up a minute later and he's still glaring at me the same way. I look down again, look up another minute later as he flicks his cigarette butt towards me – it lands a couple of feet in front of me and he's looking at me as he does it. What's all this about? All I'm doing is making everyone's day just that tiny bit brighter through my popular rendition of The Third Man Theme. What's this guy got against me? I decide I've had enough and start packing up. As I'm doing this, the guy wanders over and sort of hangs around near the entrance to Boots, just behind and to the right of me. He's shuffling around with his hands in his pockets, looking down. There's no one else about and I feel a bit vulnerable. However, just then a man comes up to me and starts talking about guitar lessons. I feel safer straight away and this other guy wanders off. No, I didn't like that at all.

Earnings: £32.43

DAY 68   Sunday March 27th 2011
           Winchester High Street, corner of Marks & Spencer
           Time: 4:38-6:20pm

Spoke for a few minutes with Frank who was, by his own admission, a bit worse for wear, having spent last night talking over old times with an old friend accompanied by a bottle of first class (VSOP) brandy, or cognac, as the French say. He then told me some stories from his misspent youth – going to the Marquee Club in London in the late '60s...

I told him about Colin and his tips for buskers – 'don't play more than 2 or 3 times a week or your regulars will stop giving you money.' Frank agrees with this – 'less is more,' he says. I still disagree – even if you don't get any money from the regular people, it's still worth coming out as most of the people I get money from have never seen me before or are from out of town.

I don't usually come in on a Sunday but there are still a lot of people about, even at 4:30, so let's see...

Well, it doesn't go that well and it's a long time before my first coin – always a depressing situation, and for some reason I am not playing well – my timing is a bit off. This annoys me, which makes it worse, which annoys me more, which makes it worse, and so on... I play for an hour and a half and accumulate only £8. I have a brighter moment when a man from Vienna – amazingly – says he likes my arrangement of The Third Man Theme better than the original by Anton Karas. I have to inform him that 'my' arrangement is in fact Chet Atkins' arrangement from 1960. I'll finish soon, I think, so cue The Good, The Bad and The Ugly! I'm playing it and can hear a man's voice from afar providing the missing bits in between the guitar bits – those monosyllabic shouts and loud grunts (!) or whatever they are that a bunch of men do from the theme. They are coming from one of a group of three – two men and a lady who are walking towards me on the other side of the pavement. The vocaliser, for want of a better word, breaks away from the group and is coming over –

'Hey! you and me – Jagger and Richards, whadaya say?!' he shouts.

'Sorry, what's that?' – I'm a bit deaf.

'Jagger Richards, Lennon McCartney – you know, we make a great team!'

'Oh yeah, Rodgers and Hammersmith, yeah, I get you!' I say, as I 'get' him.

This is Sam – a friendly man about forty-five, I reckon. He crouches down next to me – 'So how come you're here – what bands have you been in?'

'Oh, a lot – most of them, I think! But I can't do that any more…'

I give him my hard luck story – 30 years of ear abuse. It turns out that, like me, Sam has tinnitus. I tell him I've got it in both ears – the left worse than the right and my Uncle Maurice has it too – but from being blown up in the war.

'What about you?' I ask.

He points to his forehead – 'It's terrible, I hate it.'

I know how he feels. It's the worst when it's quiet, like early in the morning or late at night – when there's not much noise – that's when you notice it, or if you happen to be talking about it!

'How did you get it?'

'From DJ-ing. My sister's got it, too.'

'How so, Sam?'

'Too many Led Zeppelin gigs!'

Earnings: £23.08

DAY 69 **Tuesday March 29th 2011**
Winchester High Street
1. Corner of Marks & Spencer. Time: 1:28-3pm, 4:45-5:15pm
2. Opposite WH Smiths. Time: 3:05-4:05pm

I set up and collect £2 almost straight away, then it starts to rain. I rig down and take shelter opposite near Bertie the flowerman who again asks me where I'm from.

'I live in Greenhill Road – but I'm not *from* there. Where do you live?'

He smiles and says 'Well, Sutton Scotney – in a caravan.'

'Oh, right. I know Sutton Scotney… it's nice up there!'

It stops raining, I set up again and it immediately starts again. I can't be bothered rigging down again so quickly move everything three feet to the right, into the covered doorway of Marks and Spencer. I start playing but feel a bit self conscious and think maybe I'm not supposed to set up here – private property and all that. Just then a couple of policemen walk by and smile at me. So there you go – if they're not bothered. It stops raining again so I drag my stuff back three feet to the left. Well, one foot out then three feet left.

One of my regulars turns up smelling strongly of drink. And it's not tea. But he offers to buy me a cup of tea or coffee. I politely decline the offer.

He insists rather aggressively that I accept his offer – 'I SAID, do you want a cup of TEA?!'

I again politely decline and he storms off!

Bertie comes over – 'Do you know that guy?'

'Yeah, I see him all the time. He always wants to buy me stuff – I'm not homeless!'

After a few minutes this man comes back and although not exactly throwing, abruptly drops a sandwich – a roasted chicken and tomato panini to be precise – next to me and walks off without a word. I decide to speak to him about this later.

A young guy walks by with an instrument case – I'm guessing it's a trumpet. He stops and listens and then starts talking about busking in Chichester and Oxford – 'Oxford's the best – there's millions of people everywhere and from all over the world.'

A bit like Dudley, I think. Ha Ha!

'You can make three-hundred quid a day there.'

'Really? Where's the best place to go there?'

'Right where the HMV Shop is,' he says, causing me to wince – he has adopted the unfortunate habit currently in vogue of sounding his 'h's not as 'aitch' which is correct but as 'haitch', which is incorrect. Aitch is the name for the letter, not a guide for phonetic pronunciation, my friend!

Money-wise, I'm doing OK – about £14 in an hour and a half. Even so, I decide to move up the road for a change of scenery. I sell another of my CD albums. I have to thank Marcus for this. He bought one a few days ago and has turned up here. George, the guy in his seventies who wants to get me some gigs has turned up too. They are both sitting on the bench opposite. I don't think they know each other but I can see them start to talk and then clap after I finish a song. George then gets up and goes into WH Smiths. Marcus comes over and says he's told George about my album and he's gone to get some change and do I have a CD with me? I sure do. Meanwhile my recently aggressive drink-sodden regular has turned up.

'Look,' I say, 'I really do appreciate you wanting to buy me stuff, but I always have something just before I come out here and I don't need it – I don't want it, you're better off saving your money.'

Bertie the flowerman and his mate Darren

'Yeah, but… oh all right, I won't buy you anything any more. I'll give you money.'

'I'm not homeless, you know – I've got food!'

'No, I know. I mean you're always very presentable, you know – smart.'

'Yeah, I *do* make an effort! Thanks for noticing!'

'OK, I won't buy you anything else.'

I leave this spot just after 4 o'clock as I have to see the manager of Blanc – the posh eatery up the road, about a gig. I see the lady manager, no – they have no need of my services, not now and not at any future date. Oh well, I was going to head on home but decide to return to the noisy corner for a short session.

Before I start, I have another chat with Bertie. He reckons I need to do away with my grey beret and get a bucket for my money –

'You'll get more with a bucket. I've seen 'em all here – all the buskers, and some of them are crap. But they get a lot more people giving them money – the ones with a bucket do. Get a fire bucket or something. Y'see, people coming round the corner – a lot of them won't see your hat, but a bucket – especially if you shove it out a few feet in front of you – people haven't got to go right up to you – they can throw something in as they're walking by. It's a lot easier – and the kids love to put something in a bucket. That's only my opinion – 'cause I've seen 'em all down here and like I say, some are real crap!'

He's convinced me. I'm gonna get myself a bucket.

After I pack up, I'm walking up the road and hear a very loud, trumpety kind of sound from afar. As I get near WH Smiths, I see it's young 'haitch' – the Oxford busker. He's playing an unusual looking trumpet or cornet… or something. It's very long and it's very loud. I also see he is selling some CDs. They're propped up in his strange instrument case. But the man on the CD covers doesn't look like my haitch Oxford busker guy – the man on the CDs has long hair – haitch's hair is shorter and haitch is much younger. As I get closer, I see why – these CDs are by the million-selling instrumental artist Kenny G!

'H' is selling 'G's CDs!

Earnings: £48.00

DAY 70   **Wednesday March 30th 2011**
            Winchester High Street, opposite Clinton Cards
            Time: 2:50-4:40pm

It's that peculiar weather where it's raining but it isn't – it's drizzle, I think it's called. I take my chances and come into town. If I can get in the covered bit, I'll do an hour or so… and, yes, I'm able to get under the covered bit and the money is steady and accumulating at an acceptable rate – about £9 an hour. I'm visited by Marcus, who bought my album a few days ago. I also gave him, as a bonus, a CD of Little Speck of Blue.

'I listened to your tape (a CD), what is it? Tiny Speck… ?'

'*Little* Speck of Blue,' I correct him.

'Yeah, it's all right,' he says.

Now, there are two ways of saying 'It's all right', one is 'It's all right', the other is 'It's all right!' The first is negative, the second is positive. Marcus says it the first way.

I explode! – 'All right? ALL RIGHT?! I put EVERYTHING into my…'

I calm down mid-sentence and think – oh well, everyone's entitled to their opinion and all that rubbish. I can't be bothered and I can't be bothered quoting Mr. Van Dyke Parks' comment about the song, about MY song! I think it instead… even though he calls me 'Marv'*… and I can't be bothered to let him know that, although it's three years old now, Chris Evans played it (again) on The Curve Ball.

'Why don't you make a tape of this stuff – what you play out here? I'd give you a tenner for *that*! People would love it.'

I bet he's right – it's what people know. Oh well. Although it's not really raining… but it is, my guitar is covered with thousands of Tiny Specks of Water. 'You'll warp your guitar,' says one of my regulars as he walks by. It's the greedy man who keeps two wives. I want to tell him he'll warp something else if he keeps on like that. The water droplets don't bother me, I can just wipe them off the varnish, it's the moisture in the air that is uncomfortable – it makes my fingers sort of stick to the strings.

Marcus returns and again says he'll buy a 'tape' of me playing this stuff. I tell him he'd be better off getting a CD of Chet Atkins – he plays it better! Today marks the debut of my new collection receptacle, as suggested by Bertie the flowerman. It's not a bucket as such. It's a

---

* 'Marv's music is most marvy. Crisply arranged, winsome and winning.'

small, orange pail with a face on one side, or in other words – a child's Halloween pumpkin bucket. I've got it so the face is looking at me but I may turn it round next time – I think the kiddies will like it.

Earnings: £19.62

DAY 7I   **Thursday March 31st 2011**
Winchester High Street, corner of Marks & Spencer
Time: 2:34-5:50pm

A session of admirable length down at the noisy corner – no Bertie the flowerman, only his young helper – 'THREE FOR A PAANND!' or 'numbnuts' as Bertie calls him. To the 'happenings', as they used to say in the old days of hippiedom… An old lady racing by at three miles per hour in one of those golf carts with a roof, turns the corner, stops in front of me and puts a pound in my Halloween bucket.

'Thanks, I've never had anyone in a car stop and give me something.'

'OK, I wouldn't call this a car – it's the closest I can get though!' she says as she bombs up the road.

The weather is cloudy and windy but the temperature is acceptable so I'm able to play non-stop – and considering my ailment, playing quite well, so I make an attempt on a new number – Wheels. It's a happy tune and I want to introduce it to my set. I wait until there are about six buses lined up to go around the corner, thereby drowning out any mistakes – and there are plenty, some of which must have been heard by the two old gentlemen suddenly in front of me.

'Sorry about that – I'm still learning that one.'

One says it sounds OK to him.

The other says 'Are you good?'

'I don't know! Can you hear me?' I notice he's got a hearing-aid like mine.

'Oh yes, but do *you* think you're good?' he says. I don't often get asked this but when I do, I say 'I'm better than some and not as good as some others!' which is probably true. I play them a shortened Yellow Bird, which has the same tuning as Wheels – they like it. I ask them if they've heard me play The Third Man Theme.

'No,' says one – a dead giveaway that they're not from around here!

'Do you miss out the 1st and 2nd man?' says the hearing-aid man.

It takes a second for this to register with me.

'Sorry?'

'You just do the THIRD one?'

Ha! So, yes, I miss out the first two and play the THIRD man for them – with the wobbly/vibrato arm bits in. They like it.

The no-hearing-aid man looks at his watch – 'We'd better be off, our wives are waiting, we have to get a coach.'

I shake their hands and hearing-aid man walks away, heading up the high street. No-hearing-aid says 'He's going the wrong way.' He calls him back – 'You're going the wrong way, it's over there', he points the other way, to where the coach station is.

Later on, a woman in her mid 50s and in a hurry drops a few coins in the bucket, including a £2 coin – anything more than £2 is a big donation.

'Well, I thank you very much!' I say.

'You've caught me on the right day,' she says, out of breath. How so? 'We've just sold our house for two million – over two million. It's just gone in the account this morning!'

'That's very nice,' I say.

'Yes... (and now she says – with genuine worry in her voice – something which could easily offend many people – including me, everyone I know, everyone I've ever known and everyone who does *not* have 2 million pounds in the bank, or £200,000 or £20,000 or even £20)... but now we're HOMELESS – we've got to find another home – soon!'

Oh dear, the poor, posh, rich creature. But I'll forgive her and gladly relieve her of her £2.70 – which means less than nothing to her but is a small fortune to me.

A bit later, I relate this to Alan, the cheerful street cleaner I see every day I'm out here. We discuss the subject of enormous/obscene amounts of money and I promise Alan that if I ever win the lottery, I'll give him a nice amount.

'Can you win it soon? – I'm 75! You'll have to win it quick. Anyway, why can't they divide all that money, say if there's twenty million – why don't they give it to twenty different people and not all to one? I'd be happy with twenty thousand.' Indeed Alan – but it would defeat the purpose – it's a lottery!

Ragtime Phillip drops by to show the guitar tablature he's written out for The Third Man – he's worked it out himself but put my name in a dedication at the top 'with more than a nod in the direction of M. Carthy, L. Wijnkamp(?) and especially Marvin B Naylor – Winchester 2011.' I'm impressed he's remembered the B, but insist he adds Chet Atkins' name, as that's the arrangement I do out here, for without whom… apart from A. Karas, of course.

Near the end I play my own arrangement of The James Bond Theme. I'd played it earlier and got a few coins for my trouble. A common reaction from passers-by is the classic stance: arms outstretched – holding air gun (not a real air-gun – but like an 'air' guitar), slightly bent over, taking long strides – usually from teenagers and young blokes. This time, it's the shortish, blonde PCSO who does it. This really makes me laugh – an unusual occurrence. I think – she could do it with a real gun, or maybe they're not allowed to carry real ones, as they're not really *real* policemen/women…

Earnings: £36.24

DAY 72   **Friday April 2nd 2011**
               Winchester High Street, corner of Marks & Spencer
               Time: 3-5:45pm

A 'social' day, in that I had more than the usual number of people coming up to talk – quite often about my guitar, which is still very shiny and well kept, and asking how I am.

First up is Bertie the flowerman. He wants to know if my new 'hat' – my Halloween pumpkin bucket – is proving effective in collecting more money than my grey beret. I'd like to think it is but I'm not sure yet. It's certainly more eye catching than the beret – an orange bucket on a grey pavement stands out more than a grey hat on a grey pavement. Bertie reckons I need to move it out a bit more – another four inches, as I'm still cradling it, somewhat. He puts a couple of pounds in it.

I say 'Hey, *you* don't have to give me anything. I'll play your favourite for that,' and begin The Third Man.

'No, my favourite's Ennio Morricone, isn't it?' He's right – I'll play that next, I say.

A couple of foreign students stand in front of me –

'Play!' one says/asks/demands.

'Sorry?'

He says it again – 'Play!' I forgive him his brusqueness as he's taken the effort to use the native tongue, and play a shortened Mr. Sandman.

'Do you know this?' I ask as I'm playing. One of them nods his head. Well, I play... but they don't pay – they just walk away.

A middle aged blonde lady says or rather laughs – 'You've really brightened my day!' as she heads for the shop door. I've noticed this complimentary remark is used almost exclusively by ladies aged fifty-five and over. An old man comes up and bends down real close on my right. He wants to know all about my guitar and how I've ended up here. I tell him all about my guitar and throw in my 'hard luck story' – at no extra charge.

'And do you give lessons?'

'Yes, I do' – if I ever get the chance. I've given several people my card but not heard from anyone yet although I realise people are forgetful...

'Well, I'd like to take one of your cards, if I may. I live over there (points down to the statue)... in one of the St. John's almshouses.'

I even have a visit from Mr. Napier – chief reporter for the *Hampshire Chronicle* and the man responsible for publishing extracts from my diary way back in February. I last saw Mr. Napier clutching his newly bought DVD of The Third Man. He tells me he's had a lot of people contact the paper to say how much they liked the article. Wow! What about a follow up, I ask. Ha Ha! – I'm like Alan Partridge at his meeting with Tony Hayers, the commissioning editor of the BBC –

'What about a second series? Have I got a second series?!'

'... maybe sometime in the future – you never know where this type of thing will lead', says Mr. N, Chief Reporter for the *Hampshire Chronicle*.

Speaking of The Third Man, I become bored during one of the day's renditions and decide to vary it by playing it at different speeds, changing quickly and putting an introduction I've seen a brilliant Korean kid do on YouTube – much like the original zither arrangement by Anton Karas. I am slowly learning this alternate and quite difficult version in the hope of adding it to the set, so I will then have *two* versions to unleash on the innocent pedestrians of this fair cathedral town.

Near the end, my guitar chum, Ragtime Phillip, turns up while I'm playing my samba number – Deve Ser Amor.

'It's incredibly CHEESY, isn't it?' he says.

It sure is – cheesy (especially when I play it) and catchy, but he likes it.

Do I have the music? I do – here. He can have it.

He takes it away to photocopy it and returns a bit later. He wants to learn it – I hope he does. No repertoire is complete without a certain amount of cheese.

Earnings: £27.57

Ragtime Phillip

DAY 73   **Monday April 4th 2011**
                    Winchester High Street
                    1. Opposite Clinton Cards. Time: 2:05-4:07pm
                    2. Corner of Marks & Spencer. Time: 4:50-6:10pm

A cold and windy day means it's difficult to play certain songs – any fast bits don't come out right, so I stick to the simpler ones like Yellow Bird with which I open the 'proceedings' – and drag it out for about ten minutes at least. I've only been playing it a couple of minutes when a tall man – mid-seventies, who's been listening just behind and to the right of me comes forward – 'That song – what is it?'

   'Yellow Bird.'

   'Ah yes, but I know it as Choucoune. It was sung by a coloured chap – Henri Salvador, you know, like the country. It was called that, long before it was Yellow Bird.'

'Really?' I say. 'I only know the words are from an old poem and the melody's an old traditional one – no one knows who wrote it.'

While talking to this man, I had stopped playing Yellow Bird/ Choucoune. I now resume playing it only to be interrupted again just two minutes later, this time by another man of similar age.

'I remember that from when I was in the RAF. We were sent to the Caribbean – this was forty years ago when the Cuban Crisis had started (almost fifty years ago). They sent us out there – we flew out –'

I interrupt him here – 'What were you flying?'

'Shackletons. They put us up in a nice hotel and then forgot about us! We were there for weeks, all expenses paid! It was very nice! That song you were playing – what is it?'

'Yellow Bird' – or Choucoune!

'That brings back memories – and you think of sitting on a beach and there's that great Caribbean sunset...'

I follow his line: 'Yeah, the leaves on the palm trees swaying gently, a nice breeze, um – gently blowing. Sort of reminds me of an early Bond novel – when he goes to Jamaica.'

'Yes, well, thank you very much – it does bring back memories.'

After two hours I take a break and wander around the warmest place nearby – the HMV Shop – and check to see if my solitary album is still there... it is. I then take a very short walk and set up at the noisy (and today very windy) corner. In fact it's so windy, all my stuff's blowing about – my set list and music papers and Halloween bucket which doesn't have a flat bottom so it's wobbling/rocking about.

A couple of 19-year-olds want some AC/DC.

'Sorry, I don't do any.'

'What about some blues then,' they say.

I tell them I used to play a bit, mainly Chicago blues when I was eighteen and in Canada. I had a choice, I tell them. Either move to Chicago and play the blues, or come to England... and end up busking!

'You know any Eric Clapton? – Layla?'

Of course I do, you never forget stuff you learn when you're young. I play the high riff, then the double string one which comes in a few seconds later under the high one – my young folk love it.

I pre-empt them – 'You like Led Zeppelin? You must like some of that!'

I don't give them time to answer – they get the riff from Black Dog... but not too loud – I don't want to disturb the neighbours!

'What about some more themes?' they say – they were walking by as I was playing The Good, The Bad and The Ugly.

'Sure, you know the James Bond theme?' I'd played this ten minutes before but that doesn't matter out here.

'Yeah! Play it!' I play it, they love it – 'You're good!' They give me some money – that's what it's all about.

Earnings: £36.05

DAY 74   **Tuesday April 5th 2011**
                Winchester High Street
                1. Opposite Clarks. Time: 2:28-4:43pm
                2. Corner of Marks & Spencer. Time: 5:20-6:05pm

Like yesterday, it's cold – and although it isn't raining, it has been and there's a grey sky and the atmosphere has the moisture hanging in it which makes it difficult for playing so – like yesterday, I open with an extended Yellow Bird. One of my regulars, a very respectable looking, suited, bespectacled man, early seventies I'm guessing, stands nearby, half hiding behind the next column to the left of me, but I know he's there – oh yes – objects moving by, I don't pay any attention to but moving objects which suddenly stop – I see 'em all! This man always gives me a donation, unlike some of the regulars who are sometimes irregular with their payments... not as if they owe me anything, of course... but I like this man.

'You're draining me of my finances, you know!' he says as he puts all his change in my bucket. He likes my rendition of Yellow Bird – 'It's beguiling,' he says, smiling.

'I've heard that word before but I don't know what it means but I'll take it as a compliment,' I say.

'Beguiling? – it lifts the spirit, you could say.' I thank him, let him know who the arrangement's by and think that if Chet Atkins was still alive, I would write to him and let him know how much people enjoy his arrangements out here on the high street of Winchester, southern England.

'Do you know any Spanish classical guitar?' asks my man.

'I do – some of the easier ones, but it's too cold to play them today. Hm... do you know Choro de Saudade, by Barrios?'

He doesn't, so I start playing it but give up after a couple of bars – one wrong note and I'm finished. I apologise profusely.

My man says he '... really must attend to some business over there but thank you very much.'

I get a request from someone who's heard me before – The Third Man no less (the request, not the man). Of course I'll play it and, amazing as it sounds, I've only played it once before in an hour! The man loves it but his son at one point tries to break away and walk off – his dad holds him in front of him with both arms until I'm done. I complain about the cold.

'It's going to be twenty-one degrees tomorrow,' he says.

The money's flowing in steadily... then I get nothing for fifteen minutes, a long time when you're busking. I play Yellow Bird – the current favourite, and suddenly they all come and queue up in front of the bucket – about ten people, more or less all at once!

My friendly, complimentary, besuited man turns up again a bit later as I'm finishing The Entertainer –

'What key do you do that in?'

'I play it in D, with the low string down.'

He imitates playing a piano – 'I used to be able to play it on the piano. I'm trying to remember the key... '

'You played it on the piano?' I say.

'Yes, before my rheumatism (he holds up his hands)... had to sell the piano.'

What a shame, I think. At least with my focal dystonia, I still have one good hand and two good fingers in the other one.

Later on, down at Marks and Spencer the crowd is thinning out, it's fairly uneventful. I spend the last twenty minutes observing a young guy, possibly strung out on something. He's trying to impress his mates – a fat girl and another guy. A middle-aged woman walks by – 'Hello love, I bet you've had a few!' he says. Here's something else he does – someone walks by, he walks alongside them as far as he can until they: (a) get on a bus, (b) swear at him, or (c) hit him. I watch him inflict himself on one man: 'Hello mate, how are ya? Had a bad day?... ' I don't see him for a few minutes. His mates are laughing and looking to see if he's down the road, past the King Alfred statue. They can't see him. Then he comes back.

'How far d'you get?' his mate asks.

'Down the Abbey Gardens!' he says hysterically and they all fall about... in hysterics. I keep thinking I hope he doesn't latch on to me but I think I'm safe as he's only picking on people walking by – moving targets. At least I hope I'm safe. If not, if he comes up to me, I shall have to call out for my small, blonde PCSO to sort him out, the hooligan.

Earnings: £35.70

DAY 75   Wednesday April 6th 2011
                Winchester High Street, opposite Marks & Spencer
                Time: 1:08-2:15pm

These days I never usually busk for under an hour and a half. I often think of the days, not too long ago, when the longest 'cabaret' gig would never be longer – *and* I'd be taking home a couple of hundred quid – sometimes more, at the end of the night.

I keep forgetting that Wednesday is Market Day here in this fine town, which means it's busier – with buskers as well as shoppers. The market stalls are too close to the bit where I usually set up so I'm on the opposite side of the street, near the flower stall. Bertie the flowerman nods to me and I hold up my Halloween bucket so he can see I'm still taking his advice. I get a few donations, including Bertie. Twice he comes over in the space of a few minutes, nodding approvingly. But then… nothing. Two young women stop in front of me, one fiddles with her purse then comes up to me.

'Hello, where are you from?' I ask her, as they look foreign – very dark, almost black hair, olive complexions.

'Jordan,' she says.

'Are you just visiting Winchester?' I ask stupidly – of course they are, they're from Jordan! They ignore my (stupid) question. One holds up her camera – she wants to take a photo of her friend with me…

An old man comes up. He has a hearing-aid like me. I remember him from a while back when I was here last. He's very cheerful.

'How have you been?' he asks.

'Oh, fine, yeah, I'm OK today, I've just been…'

He interrupts – 'I collapsed in London. Heart trouble. Make the most of it – live while you can!'

Well, I'm trying to make the most of it right now but it's not going well – and the fruit and veg guy is getting on my nerves – all he seems to shout is 'REVERB! REVERB!! THREE FOR A POUND!' Surely he's not selling reverb three for a pound – they can get it from me – for free. I try and work out what fruit or vegetable sounds like 'REVERB!' Strawberries? Lettuce? Apples? Carrots? Pomegranate?… Eggplant? I give up – and pack up and I'm starting to doubt Bertie's words of wisdom concerning the world of busking. Is my orange bucket working? – I've just got £4.21 for over an hour. Oh well, I'm going to carry on using it. Who knows – I might have got even less without it. Anyway, as the song goes, I've become accustomed to its face…

Earnings: £4.21

DAY 76   **Thursday April 7th 2011**
Winchester High Street
1. Corner of Marks & Spencer. Time: 11:40-2:03pm
2. Opposite WH Smiths. Time: 2:58-3:50pm

The warmest day yet and so I change my attire accordingly – instead of my black corduroy coat, I display a black suit jacket with velvet lapels. In fact it's too warm even for that, but as I say to Bertie the flowerman before I start – 'I shall not shed it,' having never played without a jacket of some sort, ever. Alfie the keyboard busker stops for a chat. He tells me he has a friend who's been playing the Wurlitzer at a fair in Fakenham. At least I think this is what he is saying – it's so difficult to make out because of his speech impediment – and that if I'm ever up that way, I should go and visit him – he's been doing it for thirty-one years – a long fair. Alfie's a friendly fellow; I've got a lot of time for him. I just wish I could understand what he says.

A bit later, a man – one of my regulars, comes by. I haven't seen him for a while – he's become irregular.

'How are you doing?' he says.

'Fine, it's warmer so I can play a bit better.'

'I met someone who knows you, the other day.'

'Who's that?'

'Steve, I think he said.'

'Hm… and he knows me?'

'Yeah, he's pretty full of himself…'

'Oh, wait a minute,' I interrupt – I know exactly who this is – '… did he say he was one of the top eight guitarists in the country?'

'Yeah! he did, actually! He was going on and on, how good he was – in the Eclipse, at the bar. And it's one thing I can't stand – someone going on about how good they are, you know, and he was giving me all this and I said "prove it – show me, you're talkin' the talk, c'mon – show me!" and he wouldn't.'

'I know,' I said. 'He doesn't have any CDs and I asked him if he was going to record any and I got the impression he thought his music was too good for us all!'

'Yeah, well I told him about you, that I knew you and he said he knew you and he thought you were good but not as good as him! I said to him again – prove it! He started going on about his guitars and kept saying it – how great he was. In the end I had enough, I told him he could take his guitar and shove it up his arse!'

I started laughing – 'Did you really say that?'

'Yeah, I can't stand people like that, boasting – prove it or shut up, I say. I couldn't stand him, I went outside and sat at a table and he came out a bit later and asked me if there was anyone sitting in the chair beside me. There wasn't, but I told him there was and he asked me again and I said there was, and he said he couldn't see anyone and I said "there *is* someone sitting there, it's just that *you* can't see them!"'

Another regular – Marcus, drops by and we have a discussion about where they sell the cheapest batteries for my amplifier. I can get Duracell Plus quite cheap at supermarkets and petrol stations, I say. Marcus says they're cheaper at the pound shop around the corner – a pound, no more no less. Duracell Plus? Apparently. He goes away and comes back ten minutes later – and he's bought me some batteries – six of them, the right amount and the right make. Duracell… but no 'plus'.

A man who likes my Mr. Sandman rendition stops for a chat and laments the state of modern music and chat shows – 'You don't hear anything good anymore and they (TV people) just put these people on everything now, I mean, these chat shows, even someone like Alan Titchmarsh has got one. Why all of a sudden is he a chat show presenter? OK, he's a good gardener, but he's got a chat show now!' … another man, in a suit but without most of his teeth – 'Tell you what, I used to like that, um… Duane Eddy, you know, with the old four strings goin'.' FOUR strings? … I reel off what I can remember of an instrumental of his called Raunchy, basically a riff of six notes…

Time for a lunch break in the cathedral grounds. A few minutes after I sit down, a young guy sits against the tree near me and lightly strums his ukulele… I finish my crisps and small apple and get up, go over and ask him if he's ever busked with it. He hasn't – he doesn't think he's good enough. I tell him he's a damn sight better than some people I've heard and maybe he should try it. On the way out I come across a busker who I saw earlier singing Where Do You Go To My Lovely, as I was walking down the high street. This was Barry, who is with his lady-friend Sharon, from the North. Barry asks me about other good busking places. I mention Salisbury, not that I know, only someone told me it was good there recently. I ask him where he's from.

'We have a tent. We're just passing through here – Winchester, it's not bad – got a few quid, you know, with the guitar and we get a free meal, as we haven't got an address, we're entitled to one – at the Trinity Centre. We're all right if we can get a few quid – with the guitar every day.'

I do a shortish set up the road, opposite WH Smiths and think I recognise a man sitting on the bench opposite where I play. He's got a little boy next to him. I play The Third Man… afterwards he says:

'Remember me? I was really miserable and you played that.'

It's the sad man from Day 32, way back in January! I'm pleased to report that he looks better today, he has a tan and is definitely more on the cheerful side.

'You look better – is that your son?'

'Yeah – he's ten, but he looks a bit younger, yeah, it was a bad day – I change with the weather, you know.'

The weather must have been pretty bad that day – it was certainly cold, as I remember. I'm relieved something got better for him. I hope it's not just the weather… as they walk off I play The Third Man again.

An elderly man stops for a chat –

'You know what you should do? Stranger On The Shore.'

'Oh, that was Acker Bilk – did he play a saxophone?'

'Clarinet. You should do that one – it's a real money spinner,' he says. It might be for Mr. Bilk…

I've started to pack up – I've put my guitar down and switched my amplifier off when two young guys appear next to me. One wants 'some Eric Clapton or something… Cocaine – can you play it?'

Sure – an idiot could play that… and *I'm* the one who can play it now so I play the riff twice which takes 7 seconds.

'Yeah!… know any Beatles?' he says.

'Not to play on solo guitar, not really.'

'Anything, man! Know any late stuff? Revolution?'

I play the beginning – another 7 seconds.

'Yeah, man! Anything else?'

'Hmm… I know Here Comes The Sun.'

'Yeah? That's not late period though, is it?'

'Yeah, it is!' says his more with-it mate.

'Yeah, it is. It's on the last album – if that's not late enough I don't know what is!' I say as I put the capo on the 7th fret. I play the beginning.

'Sing it!' he shouts.

'I'm not a singer – I don't sing, YOU sing it!'

'No, I'm drunk, YOU sing it!'

I laugh – it's all quite amusing. 'OK, all right, I'll do a couple of lines… Here comes the sun, do do do do… ' That'll do. Farewell, my drunken man.

Earnings: £31.52

DAY 77   **Friday April 8th 2011**
                 Winchester High Street
                 1. Opposite Clarks. Time: 1:05-3:10pm
                 2. Corner of Marks & Spencer. Time: 3:58-5:07pm
                 3. Opposite WH Smiths. Time: 5:12-6:20pm

A day spent zigzagging around the high street, but that doesn't mean there was a lot of arduous travelling – the different busking places are only a minute's walk, if that, apart. My first well-wisher of the day is my nice old Italian lady, Delia. We try to have a conversation but she's got an ear infection which is giving her a lot of pain on one side of her face and she can barely hear me. She's on her way to the doctors about it. As she's about to leave, Alfie arrives, says hello and other things but it's so difficult to understand him. I reckon Delia and Alfie are two of the friendliest people I've met since I started busking.

The money is coming in steady – if it keeps up like this for the rest of the day, I'll be content.

I've got my head down and when I look up, there are two young ladies standing a few feet away, both with hands folded in front of them. I finish and they clap – a dead giveaway, they must be foreign.

'What is that?' one asks. Yes, definitely an un-English tinge there.

'It's by Bach. J.S. Bach, Johann Sebastian Bach. It's called Jesu, Joy of Man's Desiring.'

'Oh, what does it mean?'

Immediately I think of what Leo Kottke's engineer said when he was recording the arrangement I play – that Bach had so many children because his organ had no stops, but I decide not to divulge this. They probably wouldn't get it, anyway. But they might… and then they might think I'm rude.

'I don't know – it's really old, though!' I say. They ask if I know any more Bach. I tell them I don't, although I'm working on one called Siciliano which is quite difficult. I think these two look similar and I ask them if they are sisters.

'No, we just work together. We are care workers – in Edinburgh. We are going back to Germany soon. We are on our way back.'

I ask their names. They are Inga and Meret. Inga is German, Meret is Swiss. They are very friendly and they ask me if I can play any songs that they know. I can't and they don't know any of mine. Do I know Fleet Foxes? No. They do, though. I insist they play a song – they really like singing they say, and Inga says she plays the guitar. She borrows my capo – 6th fret, and they launch into a song – Tiger Mountain Peasant Song, a Fleet Foxes number and they're doing a version by First Aid Kit and I have to say that they do it very well – they sing in tune and they sing well together. I'm impressed. They sing in harmony – musically and literally. Yes, it sounds nice. When they finish, I applaud, although they seem to have been ignored by almost everyone else. I say they are welcome to sing another one but they don't want to.

I ask them about busking in their home countries – do they have buskers? They ask me what 'busking' means. A good question! I don't know.

'What do you call it in Germany?' I ask.

'Strasmusikant – street musician.' says Inga. Oh dear. The last 'a' in the word 'strasmusikant', is pronounced like a soft 'u'.

'Oh right! Oh, that sounds a bit like a swear word!' I say.

'Strasmusikant?' she says it again. 'You are a bad strasmusikant? You play some more for us?'

I play some bits from a few songs – they don't recognise any of them apart from The Entertainer, not even The Third Man. Then it's time for them to go so we say goodbye and off they go – into the shoe shop opposite.

Maurice 'The Thinker'

Before I pack up, an elderly couple stop and give me some money –

'It's good to hear some *real* music. Have you come from the stage?' she says.

Stagecoach? I might look a bit old-fashioned but I'm not quite Dick Turpin. Perhaps she's referring to my velvet-lapelled, dark (possibly stage?) jacket. She asks how I've come to be out here doing this. I give them my hard luck story. She asks me if I'm from Ireland or the West Country. I get this quite a lot.

'No, I lived in Canada for a long time.'

'Ah, that accounts for the brogue – you've got one of those Cary Grant voices.'

Cary Grant? I never get that! 'Oh, do I? I'll take that as a compliment!'

'It was meant as one!' she laughs, as they walk off.

I've been here two hours and it's time for a break – to the cathedral ground and my snack of crisps and small apple. One of my regulars, Marcus, joins me. I find out he's an artist – he has one of those big, zip up portfolio cases and he's just sold a painting. In fact he has a few on the walls of some public buildings in this town. I say I've painted a few copies of Van Gogh's paintings.

'Have you sold any?'

'No!'

For my second session I'm at the noisy corner. I'm not there very long as the money's not coming in, but long enough to run into – or have run into me, someone I haven't seen (and definitely not heard) for awhile. It's Maurice, the 'singing at the top of his voice wherever he goes' man. I see him coming towards me and remember his name just in time –

'Hello Maurice, how are you these days?'

'I'm fine, my friend! and you?'

Maurice is wearing a new looking grey vest and some black shorts which are certainly not new. His vest *is* new –

'I got two of these for five pounds. I wanted to buy some shorts. I said to the woman "Have you got a size fifty-two?" but they only had up to a FORTY-EIGHT! I said "If I wear this and I bend over, I'll be arrested for INDECENT EXPOSURE!"' I laugh at this.

'I'm going to give you some money as you remembered my name (phew!)… now, what are you going to play for me, my boy?' He doesn't wait for me to answer, he just walks off!

I go into La Vie En Rose, which I believe is what I played the last time I saw him. I hear him bellowing the melody at full throttle.

Back up the road at the old favourite, opposite WH Smiths, for a final, short spot – just over an hour. After The Third Man, an old lady gives me a coin – a £2 coin, no less.

'Well, thank you, thank you very much!' I say.

'That's all right,' she says as she half pats, half slaps me on the cheek. It's more of a slap than a pat, actually.

At 6:15 there aren't many about, apart from three druggies – two male, one female, sitting on the bench opposite me. In fact I may have unwittingly contributed to a soon-to-happen overdose. The female one comes up and asks if I have a pen. I do. 'What colour is it?' It's black – like her teeth. I give it to her. She produces a piece of paper which I can see is a prescription – there are some green sections, and she puts pen to paper, as it were. Oh well, if it wasn't my pen, it would be someone else's... or would it? Time to go, I think. This has been a very good day, nay – exceptional, money-wise. In fact, monetarily, it's been the second best day, ranking just behind the day I went up to London at the invitation of Mr. Brady. Today I took £65, including a £10 note from a regular, George – 'Good luck with the interview!' he said, noting my smart jacket. Also received – a £5 note from a young Japanese woman. All in all, a day worth coming out for.

Earnings: £65.76

DAY 78   **Saturday April 9th 2011**
              Winchester High Street
              1. Corner of Marks & Spencer. Time: 2:21-3:42pm
              2. Opposite WH Smiths. Time: 3:50-5:42pm

I don't usually play on Saturdays due to all the buskers that turn up, a lot of them from out of town. There are sometimes as many as ten, all pretty well in place by 11:30. What I usually do is take my weekly hard earned coinage to the bank. So having done that, I decided to stroll down the high street and was surprised to see not one busker! On reaching the noisy corner – Marks and Spencer – local hard working flower seller, Bertie, says hello, points to the vacant spot across the pavement and asks me if I'll be coming out today. I don't know. I've done five days in a row, my head's a bit full of it. But, as he points out, there's a lot of people about so could be a bit of money. I'm tempted, but what if Frank and his accordion turn up – he often plays there on a Saturday.

'If he's not here now, he won't be coming,' says Bertie, who knows these things. Bertie has an idea: he'll give me his mobile phone number, I can ring him up if I feel like coming down and he will tell me if there's anyone playing at the spot. What a good idea.

While I'm there I ask him how long he's been selling flowers here – 'Twenty-seven years. It's bollocks.'

Two hours later, and I'm playing my first song, and two minutes in, I've collected £11! There's a £5 note from a lady who says, 'That's for all the times I've enjoyed walking past you,' which, taken literally, sounds a bit insulting, but I think I know what she means.

I get a few more pound coins in a matter of a few minutes – good, as it's usually not more than a pound every five or six minutes. This is the noisiest time here at the corner. Along with the five or ten buses queuing to go around the corner every quarter of an hour, there seems to be a permanent group of twenty – ten young mothers with ten offspring in prams – standing, talking, shouting, screaming – and that's just the mothers, in the middle of the pavement, a few feet away from me. Then there's Bertie's 'THREE FOR A FIVER!' young mate... and me. After an hour the noise gets too much and is possibly affecting my playing – I'm halfway through Music To Watch Girls By when I have a mental block and have to stop playing – I've forgotten what comes next. I go back a couple of bars and play and have to stop again. I've played this hundreds of times and suddenly I've forgotten it! It's very embarrassing and it really scares me. Maybe I'm 'busked out' or maybe it's the noise. I hope it's the noise.

The money's stopped coming in – maybe I should move somewhere else. I've been reading Laurie Lee's *As I Walked Out One Midsummer Morning*, about when he busked with his violin across Spain in the 'thirties. One of the things he learned was not to stay in one place too long. Hmm... I think I'll move on up the road... and... it's a lot quieter here! A man asks if I know Fools Rush In.

'No, not to play instrumentally. I've got a version by Frank Sinatra at home...' It's one of those songs that has a slow, drawn out melody which I don't think translates well on the guitar.

Another person during Yellow Bird – 'My grandfather liked that.' ... another lady who works as a cashier in Boots gives me a coin. A few weeks ago I bought something and had my guitar with me, she said she had a ukulele but hadn't learnt how to play it.

'Are you learning the ukulele yet?' I ask.

'Oh, no. I'm afraid to play it when my family are about. I think they'll criticise me!' I say it's probably easier to play out here than in front of her family!

It's five o'clock and the lady with the sludge bucket prepares to do her worst. At least she warns me. Last week someone else was doing it and didn't tell me – I almost didn't escape in time. In the last fifteen minutes, a tall, well built young guy suddenly appears – 'Pasties! A pound each! Get them NOW! A POUND A PASTY!' He's the town crier for the pasty shop, complete with small bell. He's got a good voice for it, too – not too high or too low, and he's not actually shouting as such, more talking loud – his voice just has a timbre that carries well. It's bloody loud, in other words! I can hear him over my playing but stop as I feel I'm infringing on his task. He walks past me. 'A pasty for a pound! Going for a pound! I like what you play! A POUND A PASTY!'

Earnings: £28.32

DAY 79　　　　Tuesday April 12th 2011
　　　　　　　　　Winchester High Street
　　　　　　　　　1. Corner of Marks & Spencer. Time: 2:51-4:35pm
　　　　　　　　　2. Opposite WH Smiths. Time: 5:03-6:20pm

It's a slow start with not more than a meagre £2 in the bucket for twenty minutes of playing. But what's this I see – a big figure materialising from the gloom of the archway opposite. He's moving in slow motion, exiting from the mist or steam like some Hollywood action hero. It's Maurice – from the other day. He's about sixty-five, well built, bald – bullet headed with a small, military moustache... and wearing slippers. And he's seen me and he's on his way over...

'How are you my boy?! Have you made any money?!'

He takes all his change out and puts it in my bucket and sees how little there is.

'What? Is that all? That's no fucking good, is it?! COME ON PEOPLE, COME AND GIVE THIS MAN SOME MONEY – HE'S OUT HERE PLAYING FOR YOU!' he bellows at the top of his voice, as he does with 90% of what he says. 'Don't you worry, I'll get them to give you money – it'll all change now, you'll see! Come on, over here, he needs MONEY...! Come on, I'll sing a song, what shall we do?'

I suggest La Vie En Rose.

'No! I don't know all the words, come on you people, MONEY! Hear him play!'

A short Korean man walks by who Maurice knows.

'What on earth do you mean by closing down your furniture shop – you know, the one you've got up the road. People don't know where to go now! You've caused confusion and pandemonium amongst the masses!'

The poor man looks bewildered. He mumbles something. Maurice leans towards him – 'Con-fu-sion and pan-de-monium, you've caused CONFUSION AND PANDEMONIUM AMONGST THE MASSES!'

The man's wife turns up.

'Tell your husband, he's caused CONFUSION. CONFUSION AND PANDEMONIUM! etc...'

Next in the firing line – a man about fifty, hair too long, dirty suit, dirty red V-neck sweater.

'Why, HELLO my love! and how have you been? (Maurice looks him up and down) Look at your fucking suit! and what's that?' – he prods the man's jumper with his walking stick. 'You need to get that fucking cleaned, my boy!' An old man stops to put something in the bucket, one of my regulars, always well dressed, wears a flat cap, always very polite, quietly spoken.

'Hello, my sweet pea! How are you – are you going to give this man some money – oh, you have! That's more like it! Were you in the military? – you look very smart.'

'Oh yes – in the RAF,' he says, 'in 1945. We used to be called The Brylcream Boys.'

'Why was that?' I ask him.

'We were very smart – in our ties and our hair.' He taps the top of his cap.

Maurice takes over – 'In the RAF! I was in the forces, in 1963 and when my commanding officer threatened to send me to Algeria, I said "you just do that, you just DO THAT! and you'll find that I have seven relatives there, who'll welcome me..."'

Maurice's atom bomb voice attracts attention instantly and there is now a group of teenagers with us. 'All you lot, come and give this man some of your money!'

They ask me to play Moonage Daydream by David Bowie. I tell them I know the song, but not to play it. They want to see my set list.

'James Bond! Yeah, play that!'

I play it and the collective sound of me playing, Maurice's 150 decibel voice, the buses and everything else is deafening.

'And how are you?' he asks one of the teenagers – a girl with enormous breasts and very visible cleavage displayed in boob tube.

'I'm fine!' she says.

'Yes, I can see you're fine – and so can HE!' he says, nodding to one of the males in the group who's ogling away.

Another of my regulars turns up – the man who keeps promising to bring his banjo in for me to tune. He always wears one of those hats Australians wear. He's drunk and in charge of a Sainsbury's shopping bag, and leaning over. Maurice greets him –

'HEL-LOOOOOW! (He always draws out this word like someone falling off a cliff and shouting Geronimo!) my sweet pea! and how the fuck are you?!'

'I've just bought some food, I'm a bit hungry,' the man says.

'You're a bit fucking drunk as well, my sweet pea! Ha Ha!' Maurice turns to me – 'Do you know Islands In The Sun?'

'Uh, no I don't.' He belts it out in an earth shaking bass register 'THIS IS MY ISLAND IN THE SUN – WHERE MY PEOPLE HAVE TOILED SINCE TIME BEGAN – I MAY SAIL ON MANY A SEA – THE SHORES WILL ALWAYS BE HOME TO ME, then the song BEGINS! – OH, ISLAND IN THE SUN…'

'What about Ol' Man River?' I say, and start it. He starts singing.

'It's too fucking low – that's Paul Robeson!'

I try and raise the key but mess up the chords. I suggest Yellow Bird, as I detect a certain admiration for Calypso in Maurice (Islands In The Sun, after all). I start it.

'YELLOW BIRD! HIGH UP IN BANANA TREE… DID YOUR LADY FRIEND LEAVE THE NEST AGAIN, THAT IS VERY SAD, MAKE ME FEEL SO BAD!' Maurice belts it out, his hand resting on my right shoulder, his head bellowing a few inches from my ear.

'You've got a good voice, Maurice!' I say.

'I know, and once, when I was waiting for my money, I stood outside Nero's and made seven pounds in FIFTEEN minutes! That was for my breakfast!'

'That's good money for fifteen minutes,' I say. He actually told me this story a few months ago! 'Then you sang for your lunch, and then your dinner, right?'

'Yes, I did!' His mobile phone rings, he's got it set so it rings at top volume. I reckon it's so he can hear it over his own voice, wherever he is. He takes it out of his pocket, holds it high, stretches his arms wide, walks a few feet forward and opens his throat – 'SOMEBODY LOVES ME! SOMEBODY LOVES ME!!' This cracks me up, and a few people in the fallout zone, too.

Meanwhile, the drunk man has sat down just in front of me with his shopping bag and there are now two of the local tramps/beggars/drongos who walk past me several times a day – they have now joined our little gathering…

Well, this is all very entertaining and often amusing but people are avoiding the immediate area around me and not giving any money – they can't even see my orange bucket. It's just become a bunch of freaks… and I don't want to be one of them! I have to get out of here. Fortunately, some of the freaks get bored and wander off. I like Maurice, but this is becoming *his* show – The Maurice Show and not mine. After a while, it's me, Maurice and the banjo-less man on the floor, so the freak show is getting smaller – not small enough though.

Maurice has a suggestion – 'We could go travelling! I've been to France, Spain…'

Maurice wants me to see something – I have to lean my guitar against the window and walk a few feet to the right.

'See that? That's mine.' He points to a huge camper van parked just beyond the arch. 'See all those stickers on the door?' – there are lots of small stickers – 'One for every country I've been to!'

I don't really want to go travelling with Maurice, my head would explode! Eventually he goes, his voice shaking the ground and nearby buildings and leaving me with a headache.

Now it's just my drunk regular, still on the pavement. He gets a bit morose – 'I wish I was gifted, like you. I can play the banjo a bit, but not much…'

I interrupt him. 'Whoa! wait a minute, *I'm* not gifted – I just practice a lot. You just have to practice. If you want to learn how to play an instrument enough, you can do it. I tell you, it takes a lifetime, and even that's not long enough!'

He says he has a friend who plays the piano, he has 'natural talent'.

'He's still had to learn – he's still had to spend hours every day – you can bet on it,' I say. You don't learn to play an instrument by sitting down drunk on the pavement, I'm pretty sure of that, too.

I'm packed up and heading up the street to play somewhere else – if I can find a busker-less spot – and my drunk's walking next to me. He wants me to join him in the Royal Oak.

'Sorry, thanks but I've got to stay and play and I don't drink – never during the day, anyway.'

The spots at either end of the covered section are taken but I'm not going back to the corner, not today! I tell him I'm going to walk about for a bit, then maybe one of the spots will be free. I manage to shake him off – he's a nice bloke and is always friendly to me but I'm out here to make some money, however little. I'm not here to socialise! I take a toilet/small apple break for half an hour, come back and play an uneventful session opposite WH Smiths. In fact, the most interesting thing was that I was given an East Caribbean One Dollar coin – same shape as a 50p coin, by a bunch of young foreign students who were watching me from the bench. I only noticed the coin later when I was counting the money at home.

Earnings: £24.68

DAY 80　　　　**Wednesday April 13th 2011**
　　　　　　　Winchester High Street
　　　　　　　1. Opposite WH Smiths. Time: 3:25-5:15pm
　　　　　　　2. Opposite Clinton Cards. Time: 5:43-6:20pm

Got set up and started with Yellow Bird – hadn't been playing a minute when a young guy comes over – 'Can we film you for the local news?' 'Umm… yeah, sure.' I often see people doing this in the high street – whether they actually turn up on the local news is another thing. Another guy, standing in the middle of the street, starts filming me… then I think – I should be playing my signature piece – The Third Man Theme, so I ask if they mind waiting while I tune up for it, as Yellow Bird has two strings tuned down. I do this but in my haste I'm not quite in tune. Oh well, I play The Third Man for about twenty seconds… then The First Man comes over, says thanks and puts a couple of coins in the bucket.

I'm having a lot of tuning problems during this set. In fact I'm having to check all the strings after almost every song, which is time consuming, tedious and boring for us all…

A man – listening, slightly behind me and to my side, presents himself – 'So, what guitarists do you listen to?'

'Hm… probably Chet Atkins – for the stuff I do out here, anyway, but I've listened to loads of others in the past.'

He tells me who *he* likes – 'I like Peter Green. Before he went weird, and Al DiMeola – I've met him and written to him, a few times. Actually wrote back to me – a letter. He's a really nice man.'

'Really?' I tell him about when I sent emails to a few well known pianists and fingerstyle guitarists to ask if they had ever heard of or knew anyone with my focal dystonia hand condition. The only one who bothered to reply – within half an hour! – was Roger McGuinn, my 12-string guitar hero from way back when.

'What's focal dystonia?' the man asks.

'It's a neurological condition where the signals from the brain get confused and mixed up on the way down to the hand, etc…'

He interrupts – 'Neuroplasticity.'

'What's that?' I say. He reels off a load of words containing, on average, eight syllables. He writes down the name of a specialist, a 'pioneer' on the subject, which I say I'll investigate – and many thanks, sir.

Back on the topic of friendly, famous musicians, the man tells me that, now, if you want to go backstage and 'meet the band', you have to pay – money.

'Not like in the eighties,' he says, 'when *they* were glad to see *you*. I had to pay one hundred and fifty pounds for three of us, to go backstage the other day in Portsmouth.'

And who was that, I ask.

'The Moody Blues – but they're all like that now. AND there was only three of them – John Lodge, Mike Pender and (The Third Man whose name I've forgotten). No, not like it was in the eighties…'

A bit later a man comes up – dirty, dark suit, black Stetson, necktie, sandals, slurring his words –

'I wanna form… a baaaand, y'know, gotta get an amp, guitar… people say I should do it, y'know… I look like, um… I should be in a baaand (Motorhead, maybe)… yeah… I done the drugs, been through thaaat… yeah…'

Oh dear. I tell him it's a lot of hard work (sometimes). I look down and see his big toenail, which looks like it's got a horrible disease, like gangrene. Anyway, he drifts off, to form his band – in his mind, I expect.

At the end, for my final two songs, I'm joined by an old acquaintance from the open-mic days – young Bethyn, who takes off her purple boots and dances in the more or less deserted street. Certainly, the calm after the storm that was yesterday.

Earnings: £24.00

DAY 81

Thursday April 14th 2011
Winchester High Street
1. Opposite Clarks. Time: 2:15-3:20pm
2. Corner of Marks & Spencer. Time: 3:37-6:25pm

I play for just over an hour at my first spot and just a few minutes in a young lady of about 20 runs up and puts her mobile phone right in front of my amplifier – it's The Third Man of course! – then returns to whoever it is she was talking to. I've never had *that* before, possibly never again – it must sound like an old record to the person on the other end. On the opposite side of the pavement are five workmen up to their knees in a hole of their own creation and just big enough for them all to fit in. They're not drilling or doing anything loud, just standing still then walking around a bit scratching their chins and arses. So, I provide their background music for a while then start to pack up.

A regular pops up – a man in his late sixties, white hair, always has a cheeky smile.

'Had a good day?' he asks me.

'Yeah, not too bad – got about eight pounds for an hour out here.'

'Yeah? A bit cold though, isn't it?'

'It's OK, it's not like it was a couple of weeks ago – I don't want to do another winter, I'm too old for it!'

'Ever tried busking in Paris?' he says.

'No. I'd like to, though. I reckon I could go to a lot of places now – you know, having done this a few times now, and people know The Third Man all over the world!'

'You'd be getting Euros instead of pounds, you know – and they're eighty-six pence to the pound.'

'Hm, yeah, that's a good point – and a pound coin is the usual acceptable amount to give a busker.'

'AND, it's an expensive place to live,' he says.

'Yeah, it is, although you can live in cheap places, like anywhere else. I stayed in a really cheap place a few years ago when I went to Paris – near the Bastille. When I opened the curtains there was a concrete wall three feet away!'

Down at the corner I'm visited by the sad old French lady who's always in the same long velvet burgundy coat. She very rarely smiles. I always play La Vie En Rose for her and she always sings the first two lines – nothing more. Today I find out her name – Marie-Thérèse. She has a guitar but doesn't play it because it hasn't been tuned for six months and it's gone out. I say I'll tune it for her – she's written her address out for me. She's not very well. She has something strapped to her waist which monitors something or other and she has to live in 'sheltered housing' – a term which always confuses me!

About an hour later I notice a little girl dancing – or jumping wildly with both arms and legs flying out. She's at the other side of the pavement, 'dancing' and looking at me. She's with her mother, who tries to drag her away after a couple of minutes – which she eventually does, but soon returns to continue her dance.

Her mother shouts: 'She's doing musical shadows!'

What's that? I'm playing The Third Man and whenever there's a stop in the music, she stops dancing so I decide to develop this by playing The James Bond Theme and doing a musical chairs thing – I will stop playing, abruptly in unexpected places – which I do and we have a good time, both of us. It's quite fun even for me! (Things were getting a bit boring out here.) After I finish, she drags her mother over to me and I get a pound.

'That was good,' I say. 'What's your name?'

'Charlotte. I want to sing a song!' – How did I know she might say that?

'OK, Charlotte – which song? I might not know it, you know!'

'You Are My Sunshine – I'll start singing it and you join in,' she orders.

So I do as she says, and she's in the key of C and I just manage to keep up with her. We finish and a couple of people around us clap and one old lady gives some money – to her, not me! How old is Charlotte?

'I'm five but I sing like I'm six or seven.'

Would she like to do another song? Of course she would. Which one? Eternal Flame by The Bangles. Thanks a bunch. Oh well, I do my best but I haven't got a clue of the chords, of which there are many more than three. I embarrass myself – as I do with her *next* selection, Away In A Manger. I think my brain's busked out. But she's very sweet (of course!) and I even give her two 5p coins from my hard earned collection!

'Well, Charlotte (I shake her hand), it's been a pleasure – for you! Just kidding, it's been a pleasure meeting you. Next time we'll do You Are My Sunshine again, key of C.'

They go off, Charlotte waving and 'dancing' all the way.

It's The Third Man again! and a regular, an old man I met last week (he was enquiring about lessons) comes up and wants to know how long it would take him to learn it. I say I would have to hear what he can play and see how good he was.

'A few weeks, do you think?' he asks.

'I don't know – maybe. Do you know this technique? – fingerstyle, with the bass, chord voicing and melody – you play them all at once.'

'No.'

'Well, it's a good technique to learn, but it *does* take a while. I can play *this* OK, but I've played this a million times, or near enough!'

'How long would it take *me* to play it?' he says.

'Well, like I said, I don't know. The thing is, it sounds quite simple doesn't it? (I play a bar)… but there's a few things going on at once – you've got the bass bit, on the low strings which you have to mute with your right hand palm, so it sounds a bit like a string bass, soft-like, then you've got the chord notes, which you have to play short and staccato-like, then you've got your melody, but you have to play *that* legato, smooth-like, with different fingers of the same hand… ' I demonstrate all three parts separately, then all together.

'Yes, how long do you think it would take me?'!

Too bloody long.

It's six o'clock and I notice another regular, 73-year-old Mabel crouching over a drain cover near the bench nearby. It looks like she's inspecting something or dropped something down it. She moves to the one a few feet in front of me and I can see her put her fingers in the little square holes – removing any obstructions.

She comes over, so I ask, 'Why are you doing that, Mabel?'

'Well, someone's got to do it. I've done them all up the street – they're filthy, look!' She shows me her hand, her fingers are black with grime and filth and who knows what.

'Are you going to wash your hands?'

'Well, I was going to go to Sainsbury's – to the toilets there.'

I tell her they don't have toilets there, not for us civilians, anyway.

'Don't they? Well, I don't have a tissue.'

I give her a handkerchief, monogrammed with an 'M', no less.

'I'll clean it and give it back to you tomorrow,' she says.

Mabel, you have had a varied life indeed – author of six books, one translated into a foreign language, teacher, and now… cleaner of dirty street grilles. That's just not right…

Just before I pack up, an old man fiddles with his wallet a few feet away. He comes up, gives me a pound, I thank him and ask if he knows the song.

'No, very nice, though. What is it?'

'It's called Yellow Bird.'

'Is it? Oh yes – very nice. Key of A, it sounds.'

'No, almost though – it's in G.'

'Really? Sounds like A.'

'You must be a musician – guitar?'

'Oh no – piano – well I used to play.'

I then ask him what I ask all piano players I meet –

'Did you play any Chopin?'

'Oh yes, a little.'

I tell him I play some of the Preludes – the easier ones.

'Oh yes.'

He still thinks my Yellow Bird is in A, even when I insist it's not – 'It *would* be if I put my capo on the second fret (I do this), see, *now* it's in A, but (taking the capo off) now it's in G.'

'Hm… sounds like A!' he says.

This man is very well spoken, cleanly shaved and had made an effort to dress well with suit, tie, hat with a small feather, nice coat and expensive looking shoes, but it all looks very old and worn and the stitching on his shoes is coming away. I wonder how he has come to be like this. Hmm… I wonder. He says goodbye and walks around the corner. I think; he must know The Third Man – he's at least eighty. I'll tune up quickly and play it. I do and a minute later he reappears –

'Goodbye', he says, walking off, his hand waving at me.

Earnings: £36.13

DAY 82   Friday April 15th 2011
               Winchester High Street, opposite Clarks
               Time: 2:35-6:25pm

On inspecting the goings on in the high street, I find Frank down at the corner – at the bottom end, and a young strummer in the middle – at the bottom end of The Pentice. That leaves only one place for me to go, which is fine, as one place is all one needs. Before I set up, I chat to the sad French lady – Marie-Thérèse, who's sitting on a bench. She bemoans the impatience of the local taxi drivers, tells me she was a qualified nurse for fifty years and was married to an accomplished musician.

So, almost four hours in the same place – just like the bad old days at Southampton and the cold months here. Same spot as yesterday, and the five workmen from yesterday are here but making a lot more noise today – there's an intermittent drill, but it's not too intrusive on my playing time, so I needn't go over and have words. My very smartly dressed man, late sixties, who I often see, always generous with coinage and compliments, comes up.

'I'll have to become a tax exile! – giving you all this money every time I see you!'

I thank him very much – 'You're very generous!'

After La Vie En Rose, an old couple come up.

'It's great to hear someone play that here!'

'Thanks, it's a Chet Atkins arrangement.' I always tell people that as it's not one of his better known recordings.

'Ah yes,' the man says – 'We saw him at the Albert Hall in sixty-six. We hadn't been married long, had we?' he turns to his wife.

'No, in the early days, it was,' she laughs.

'Wow, and that was a great period for him, some great recordings around then.'

'Yes, I've been listening to him years – got twelve albums!'

'Right, well I'm afraid I'm going to trump you on that – I've got about thirty-five!'

'Well, he made a lot – over a thousand tunes, apparently.'

'Yep, I know he made over one hundred albums – *and* he is the most recorded musician – *ever*!' (No one's going to out-Chet me!)

'Yes, and he turned country music right round – did all those albums with Jim Reeves, produced him…'

'Yep, *and* produced Elvis – played guitar on Heartbreak Hotel!'

Marie-Thérèse

'Yeah, and did that album with, what's his name… Knopfler.'

'I haven't heard that one.'

'One thing he couldn't do – sing!'

'Oh, I don't know – he had a good country voice, I thought.'

'Thing is, all these young people – the musicians, don't know about him.'

'No, I agree – mind you, when I started out playing the guitar – when I was a lot younger, I didn't play this fingerstyle stuff. I didn't even know about it, never heard of people like Chet Atkins. I was playing all that blues stuff… (I play a fast, boring blues guitar passage) that's what all young players do when they start out and most of them just carry on doing it till they're, well, my age! I've heard them in the guitar shops, here, in London, everywhere. They do it 'cause it's easy, that's why you hear it everywhere, but you can't play stuff like that out here – just a guitar solo! It sounds crap. It's not like any Chet Atkins stuff, which sounds easy – some of it! But you try and learn it, there's loads of things going on. It's easily as hard as any classical guitar or Spanish guitar. I know! I've been doing some of his songs for years and I still really struggle.'

Just after this nice couple go off, I've got my head down, playing Jesu, Joy of Man's Desiring and when I look up, who should be standing, or rather dancing in front but the small hurricane of yesterday – it's Charlotte, age five! She's adjusted her tempo according to the tune so it's the same dance as yesterday but in slow motion.

I finish and she asks me 'Are you going to play another one?'

'For you? Sure.' Charlotte gets The Third Man… and she dances away to this fun tune and then her mother drags her away. Two meetings with Charlotte in as many days – it's more than an innocent busker can handle.

There are a few large groups (or packs?!) of foreign students out today – one stops to listen to me, respectful for the most part – there are a few noises of impatience – I'll ignore them. When I finish the song I'm playing, many of them step up and contribute to the cause with cold, hard coinage. I'm thanking them and looking in the bucket as they are pouring their coins in. HARK! – I see an unfamiliar shaped coin lying there and notice three of the boys who have walked off, laughing hysterically and looking back at me. No, I'm not having this. I do something I've never done before – I call a contributor back.

'Whoa! Wait, come back!' I shout, not too loudly, and hold my arm out, extend my forefinger then slowly curl it back towards me – twice.

They return, smiling but not laughing. I pick up the alien coin and hold it out to one of them – they're 14/15 years old, I reckon.

I say slowly 'I CANNOT TAKE THIS COIN, THE BANK WON'T TAKE IT. YOU HAVE TO GIVE ME ENGLISH MONEY, ONLY ENGLISH COINS… PLEASE.'

I'm not sure they understand me but I think they do, because, in what I take as a collective gesture of apology, they ALL now put money in the bucket, many of them making sure I see the money they're putting in *is* English money, and I'm pleased to see a great many pound coins – the best kind of coin, apart from the sacred, scarcely donated £2 variety. When they've all given, I say a big thank you and ask where they're from. I have to ask three times before a voice says 'Czech Republic.'

'Ah,' I say, 'and when are you going back?'

No answer. Anyway, in the end, all tolled up, they gave me about fifteen pounds. And yet they still managed to get one of their own coins in there, past my eagle eye. It's a 5 K(?) silver coin, very similar to a fifty pence piece, found later on at home. Still, I'm grateful to my cheeky Czech friends – they jacked my total to just over sixty pounds. Without them, it would have been about forty-five…

Earnings: £62.18

DAY 83

Sunday April 17th 2011
Winchester High Street
1. Opposite Whittards. Time: 2:05-4:45pm
2. Corner of Marks & Spencer. Time, 5:25-6:03pm

After donating to the cause yesterday, a friendly man informed me that there was an arts and crafts market in the high street today and as a consequence, a lot of people about. So, having had a day's rest on Saturday, I decided to come out. I busk every day of the week but, as the song goes – 'Never on a Sunday.' A stroll down the high street reveals all – Rob is in place at the top at the Buttercross – famous Winchester meeting place. He says 'Hello Marvin!' through his PA. He's come up from Fareham for this. Halfway down a couple of girls are singing and down at the other end, Frank's taking a break. Or giving his accordion one… and everyone else. Ha! 'Too late' is all he says to me. It's OK, I can set up around the middle of the covered bit.

First up is a poor lady of about seventy who's had her shopping trolley stolen.

'I just want to crawl into a field and go to sleep and forget about it...'

Oh dear, I say, has she phoned the police?

'My son's looking after it all, but, you know, he's a busy young man, he's got other things he has to do...' She says she's on her way to the bank.

That's a good idea... but it's Sunday, they won't be open will they?

'Yes, I'll have a walk up there, anyway... just want to crawl in a field...'

I ask if she has food.

'Oh, yes... well, I'd give you some money, but I can't...'

A bit later, it's my inebriated, hatted regular from last week, and in a similar condition today only he has exchanged his Sainsbury's bag for a painting – a vista of a small fishing town's harbour under a cloudless sky, from what I can make out through the bubble wrap. He sits on the bench opposite, listens for a bit, then comes over, puts a ten pound note in the bucket and says 'I'm not trying to stop you but will you play Harry Lime for me?' Sure, I say, but that's a lot of money, does he want some change? – I can give change. He tells me to shut up! I played Harry Lime, aka The Third Man, a few minutes ago but for this – sure, I'll play it as many times as he wants! If people don't like it, they can come and pay me to stop.

He leans against the pillar next to me and listens. He really loves this tune – it's 'heaven' he says. When I finish, he asks me about my 'background in music... what did you start off doing – Bobby Darin? Chuck Berry? You've obviously been playing a long time.'

I tell him it's more Chet Atkins – for the solo stuff I do out here.

'Oh right, d'you do the boom, chk, boom chk...' (makes sound like the Merle Travis picking technique, the alternate bass notes, etc.)

'Yeah, in fact that's what I do on The Third Man – that's a Chet Atkins arrangement' – I do a bar of the boom, chk, boom chk thing he was going on about.

He goes back and sits on the bench. I can see him trying to convert a young lady sitting there. She gives me a quizzical look, looks back at him then leaves. He comes over again. This time he's pulled out a, gulp – TWENTY POUND NOTE! Oh my, is this also to be mine? Yes it is! I again offer change for his precious note. He again tells me to shut up. This is a lot of money – with the ten pounds he's already given me, this is what I'd normally make in a three or four hour session, on a good day.

'Look, I'm not being flash but I've got money to burn.' (Don't do that – give it to me!) 'I've just bought that painting over there (points to bench with painting) for three hundred quid.'

I thank him profusely – how else? He returns to the bench, next to a little girl who's sat down while we were talking. He's talking to her, takes off his hat, revealing bald head – 'You see, I'm strange – I've got no hair on top, but hair at the bottom (his beard)... ' He comes back over. He's decided he would like me to play for two hours at his sixty-fourth birthday party in a nearby pub sometime in July and he would like me to play The Beatles song When I'm Sixty-Four, because he will be, yes... sixty-four. He says I don't have to but it would be nice if I would. He's willing to pay me the same amount I'd get if I was still doing those old 'cabaret' gigs, which is an enormous amount compared with what I get for two hours out here. Do I agree to his 'fee'? Of course I do! I'll do my best with the song request, too.

Three fifteen-year-olds come up while I'm playing. I've had enough of them already!

'D'you play Sweet Home Alabama?'

'No, try the guy up the road – Rob, he plays it, I'm pretty sure.'

'Why don't you play it? What do you play?'

I nod my head to the ground next to me –

'Have a look at that list.' I doubt if they can read. They don't know anything – on the list and literally. But I am patient and accommodating and willing to treat them to a burst of Whole Lotta Love or the torturous, complex riff of Black Dog.

'What about Led Zeppelin?' I say. Well, they just look at me with contempt and walk off. Good, be gone with you, foolish young humans.

I have a pleasant hour playing and receiving compliments from many passers-by and people on the bench, taking a break. Some even clap. However, the mood's about to change. I'm playing The Third Man Theme when a tall, unkempt, baseball-capped man walks past and says, or rather shouts, 'Don't you play anything else? You're always playing that, every time I walk by!'

I see red, stop playing and stand up.

'Yeah, I play it because people like it!' – they do – some even think it's 'heaven' when they hear it! That one guy did, anyway.

'How many songs do YOU know?' I shout.

'What?' he shouts back.

'HOW MANY SONGS DO YOU KNOW?'

'Well, hundreds,' he says.

'Well, you come out here and sit down here and fucking play them, then!' I shout.

He walks off, shaking his head – I hope he shakes it till it drops off. I've been waiting for something like this to happen, actually. I'm bound to annoy at least one person – maybe he's been walking by *every* time I've played it, just through coincidence. I've had it pretty easy, as far as being left relatively untouched by insults. I'm always having people coming up saying how much they like what I play – and the other day, when I went into Clinton Cards before I started, to say I'd only be playing an hour or so – so I hope I wouldn't annoy them, the young guy said he actually *wanted* me to busk outside. So, I've had it good and can't complain and anyway you can't please all the people all the time, etc. It did made me think, though. I'm out here, more or less forcing this music on thousands of people I don't know – that's just the nature of it. I don't know what mood any of them are in unless they decide to let *me* know. I don't worry about the old people or the people with children or the women, just the lone male in his twenties and thirties, like the guy on the bench the other week who flicked his cigarette at me. It's only then when I feel vulnerable. I'm also a bit annoyed with myself reacting the way I did as I don't like to swear in front of innocent people but, thankfully, there weren't many about. Oh well, I take it this guy won't be joining any fan club of mine.

After a couple of minutes, I simmer down and carry on. A man from the art stall nearest me comes over – he's packing up now and he wants to thank me – 'We really enjoyed listening to you.'

'Well, thanks! Are you going now?' (I see loads of paintings stacked up.) 'Was it you that sold the painting to that guy – you know, who was hanging around me for ages?'

'Oh him, yeah!'

I pack up and head up the road. I stop at the Buttercross, where Frank is – 'Going already?' he says – it's just past five o'clock. I tell him about my number one fan. With sixteen years of busking behind him, Frank's heard them all.

'Well, I've heard them all. I get people throwing pennies, and saying "That's for the dog," then they snigger, you know, and walk off, or they say "play a PROPER song."'

Frank's dog Kazoo has been in a fight. She has a wound on the top of her leg which looks very bad, it has about ten stitches and she's wearing one of those cone things to stop her licking it. On it, people have written things like 'The lady with the lamp shade' and 'Get well soon'.

There are still a few people about so I decide to head on back down to the corner and do a final, shortish session – not more than an hour, though. I might pick up ten quid. I've noticed that it doesn't matter if there are thousands of people about or only a few – I seem to end up collecting about the same amount, strangely enough. I want to visit the toilet before I start so, on getting to the bottom of the street I turn right to go through the arch.

A few feet from the entrance to the toilets there is a middle-aged man lying on his back. I think he's on a stretcher and there are two ambulance guys bending over him and saying 'Roger, Roger?!' However there's no movement from him, whose name I'm assuming is Roger. I look at his chest and it doesn't look like he's breathing.

I walk past all this and up the stairs to the toilet. I'm thinking, what if this man's dead? Maybe he'll be there for a while, I mean, there'll be no rush to get him to the hospital, will there? Can I really play The Third Man when there's a dead body lying nearby? This isn't Vienna in 1949. There's no black market racketeering going on. It's not even a film set. This is Winchester 2011, just after the arts and crafts market.

Then I think of the scene in the Marx Brothers film when he's taking the man's pulse and he says 'Either this man's dead or my watch has stopped!' and I start laughing and then I feel guilty. When I come out, the ambulance men seem to have propped up 'Roger' so I think he's going to be OK. Well, one of them says 'I think you've had a few too many sherries, Roger', which is a bit of a weird thing to say to a dead man, so I'm guessing he's all right.

It's been a profitable day. Without the thirty pounds from my hatted man, I would have taken just under a tenner an hour – an acceptable rate – so it was definitely worth coming in, despite an assortment of foreign coins cheekily finding their way into the bucket – one American dime (10 cents), a five Euro cent from Italy, a five Euro cent from the Netherlands, a gold twenty Euro cent from somewhere without a name and six Euro cent coins from a place called Letzebuerg.

Earnings: £69.65

DAY 84   Tuesday April 19th 2011
                  Winchester High Street
                  1. **Opposite Clarks. Time: 1:45-3:25pm**
                  2. **Opposite WH Smiths. Time: 4:50-6:40pm**

I've just sat down and tuned the guitar when one of my regulars turns up.
He says he's seen our friend Marie-Thérèse, the long burgundy coated
French lady.

'Oh yes, she wants me to go to her house and tune her guitar,' I say.

'Ah, that's what she's calling it now, is she! I didn't even know she had
a guitar!'

'What?' Then I get the drift of his insinuation. 'Um, NO! I said I'd
go round and tune her guitar for her – it was *me* who asked *her* for her
address!'

'Oh… well, I'm just warning you, watch out! And she'll probably be
drunk, too,' he says.

'Right, OK, thanks.'

I begin with several songs with the two lowest strings lowered two
semitones. So it's Yellow Bird – always a good 'starter' song, as it's not
too difficult to play and very mellow, followed by Wheels which is much
more difficult with my focal dystonia, and then an untried/untested
tune – a mid-seventies Chet Atkins arrangement of Vincent – 'Starry,
Starry Night… ' by Don McLean. It's a really famous tune and should
bring in some coins… if I can play it right – there are some complicated
sections, with harmonics but I've practiced it a lot at home… I play for
fifteen minutes before I get, or 'earn', my first coins: two 20s and a 10,
during the new song, so that's OK. A man of about sixty drops three 2p
coins in and seems genuinely proud of his donation – 'See? Three 2p
coins, see… ' he says this before he puts them in *and* after – picking them
up again and showing me. I think there's something not quite right about
him but thank him very much anyway. Halfway through the set I glance
to my left and see the familiar hulk of Maurice sitting on the bench near
WH Smiths. I can *hear* him, in fact! I get back to concentrating on my
playing.

The workmen from last week are here again, in their hole. They're a
bit noisier today – they've got what I can only assume is a saw for sawing
concrete – a concrete saw, I reckon. It's loud, but they don't use it all
the time, and then only for a couple of minutes. Even so, it's getting
on my nerves and I decide to move after an hour and a half, which is
long enough to be playing in one place anyway but the workmen are all

right – one was whistling along to La Vie En Rose earlier. Before I go, a man with his eighteen-month-old daughter listens. He gives her a coin and tries to get her to put it in my bucket but she just wants to hand it to me. After several tries I take it, put it in the bucket then take out a 1p coin and hand it to her as a gift. She takes it and puts it in the bucket! I feel sorry for her – she looks like she's had an operation on her eye and has a patch over it. She doesn't make a sound the whole time – I really do wonder what's going through the minds of these really young children when they hear this weird sound coming from this man with a guitar, a small black box beside him and an orange bucket in front of him.

I try and relax for a few minutes in the cathedral grounds – eat my small apple and read a couple of pages of a book I've brought with me, James Bond – *Live And Let Die*. However, it's difficult to read if I'm not relaxed, and I'm not, as I'm not here to read books! I'm here to busk and feel guilty reading, so I probably won't bring a book again!

Back at the high street I can see Maurice is still there. I have to make a decision: do I set up where he is and risk him engaging me with the probable negative consequence to my earnings, or do I set up further down and have a relaxed, financially predictable second session? I take the wrong decision and set up near him, opposite WH Smiths. I'm tuning up and can hear him greet me from *inside* the pasty shop which is behind me and up a bit. He comes out, stands next to me.

'I hear Zeta-Jones has joined the club! She's decided to come out, oh yes! Bi-polar! Oh yes, my boy, I'm in good company – Stephen Fry, Winston Churchill, what's his name… the chap who painted the flowers…'

'Van Gogh?' I say.

'Yes, him too!' He prods my bucket a few inches further out towards the pavement with his walking stick and shouts out to anyone: 'COME ON PEOPLE! ARE YOU GOING TO GIVE THIS MAN SOME MONEY?! HOW'S HE SUPPOSED TO BUY FOOD?!'

Maurice tells me of his new business venture, selling fruit and flowers in a lay-by up the A43 near Silverstone.

'And I'm going to get a man to install a refrigeration unit in my camper, and you know why, don't you… because as the mums are buying the strawberries and the flowers, the kiddies are going to want an ice lolly, aren't they?'

Maurice says his fruit is delicious and, being amiable, I say I would like to try some sometime.

'Would you? Well, come with me, it'll only take a minute – we just have to walk through Boots and my van's on the other side! You can leave your things with them in that shop, they won't mind – if you ask them nicely, or I'LL ask them, I'll TELL them, they won't refuse ME, Ha Ha!'

I say it's OK, it only takes me a minute to pack up – I'll take it with me. I haven't even played a note and I'm packing up! But wait, Maurice has sat down again and is feeding a dog cream from a pastry. He's scooping the cream from the pastry and the dog's licking it off his fingers. Five minutes later, he gets up then sees someone he knows, because he knows EVERYONE, of course. It's a man with one leg in a wheelchair. He's telling him about his fruit. A few minutes later we finally start walking through Boots.

'Does that man want to try some of your fruit, too?' I ask Maurice.

'Oh no! He likes BEER! That's why I call him Legless Brian!'

While walking from one side of Boots to the other, Maurice talks to no less than three more people. He sees a woman with a baby in a pram.

'My she's getting BIG!' Then, to the baby – 'aren't you? How old is she now – six months?'

The mother: 'No, six weeks!'

We get out the other side and Maurice is talking about his bi-polar condition. 'My doctor says people like me think they can rule the world! I said, well I CAN rule the world! Churchill had it – how d'you think he shot up all those Huns?'

We get to his camper and he opens the side door. 'You know, it used to smell real ARSEHOLEY in here, but now I've got it smelling lovely! Come over here, put your nose in!' I do, it's full of little trays of fruit and flowers and paintings…

'Yeah, it's very nice, Maurice – has a nice sweet smell.'

He gets back in and hands me two small bags of plums – 'Here, you give this to my nice tailor in that shop.' He was talking to the obviously well-dressed man from the Gieves and Hawkes shop when we got to his van, parked right outside the shop. 'Say it's from Maurice, with his regards!'

I do this. Back outside, Maurice is in the driving seat. The seat next to him, like the rest of his van, is covered with fruit, books, flowers, paintings… He talks some more of his A43 business concern. I tell him it reminds me of the Somerset Maugham story *The Verger*. Does he know it? No he doesn't – this gives me a chance to speak! I tell him the basics of the story, about a man, the verger of a church who's called into the office when it's discovered he can't read or write. The priest/vicar can't have an 'illiterate' working here so they sack him from his job which he's done for years. On walking home, he feels like a cigarette but there's no tobacconist. He reckons he can't be the only one who would like there to be a tobacconist here, so he gets all his money and opens one himself – which becomes successful, so he goes around and finds another street that could do with having a tobacconist and opens one there, then does the same in many other streets, and eventually he has a whole string of them and becomes rich. One day his bank manager calls him in to his office and suggests he invest some of his fortune. He agrees and is given some forms to read and sign. He tells his bank manager he can't read or write.

His bank manager says 'You mean to tell me you've built up this very successful business and you can't read? Good God, man, where would you be if you *could* read and write?!'

'I can tell you – I'd be the verger of St. Peter's Church,' the man says.

I eventually end up back in the high street and begin playing about an hour after I set up the first time. I have an uneventful session. For the last half hour I listen to three young guys, one quite fat, sitting on the Buttercross making loud comments to people walking by. They then walk past me, the fat one saying 'We'd give you some money mate, but we ain't got any right now. Haha!'

Money-wise I've had a lousy day – only twenty-three pounds and I've been here for *five* hours, although I've been playing for no more than four – my own fault. However it's always entertaining whenever Maurice is around and the two bags of plums he gave me are very nice.

Earnings: £23.15

DAY 85   **Thursday April 21st 2011**
            Winchester High Street
            1. Opposite Clarks. Time: 11:15-1:15pm
            2. Corner of Marks & Spencer. Time: 1:25-4:20pm

A warm, sunny day and a long session with the only break occurring when I moved from one pitch to the other. Before I set up I take a stroll down the street to see who's where – today there's no one anywhere. I decide not to set up, down at the corner, because it's too hot! This is the only spot I play at which isn't in the shade, all the others up the high street are shaded by the tall buildings on the opposite side of the street.

I'm a few songs in and have just finished La Vie En Rose when a couple in their sixties, listening on my left, come forward.

'You play well, but you look so unhappy! You should smile!' says the man.

'Well, I'm not unhappy, I'm just concentrating. There's a thin line between being unhappy and looking concentrated, maybe. And my eyes have always been a bit sensitive to sunlight – they only usually let me out at night, you see!'

After I play The Third Man, another sixties man comes up – 'That was played on a zither, wasn't it? Who did that?'

'It was Anton Karas – yes, on a zither,' I say.

'Yes, and do you know I heard him play in a place in Boscombe about five years ago.'

'Anton Karas? In Boscombe? Five years ago you say?'

'Yes, about that – maybe a bit longer, but my god he could play!'

Well, he *must* have been good – especially good to play in Boscombe five years ago – he'd been dead for twenty!

The workmen are here again in their hole and getting noisier by the day. The concrete saw is being switched on more than usual and they're not waiting for me to finish a song before they switch it on, which I think is rather rude and I'm becoming annoyed so it's time to move – I've been here two hours anyway. Before I move down the street I chat to the young guy sitting on the bench opposite holding the Asgard tattoo shop sign.

'Are you here all day?' I ask.

'No, I do four hours and three tomorrow. It's not too bad – I get a fiver an hour.'

Even I get more than that, usually!

'Then what do you do, do you go somewhere else and hold it (the sign)?'

'Oh no, I go home and go to bed.'

I go down to Marks and Spencer – there's a nice breeze now – that's good, it won't be too hot. If it's too hot my fat fingers get even fatter and it's uncomfortable and difficult to play. So, it's been too cold for four months and now it's going to be too hot. Typical. Ten minutes after leaving the first spot and I'm playing again. The security guard from Marks and Spencer comes out and says a nice thing to me. He's heard the rumour about the license or permit all buskers will have to get, to play in Winchester. He thinks the police want to get rid of us and he's been talking to the blonde PCSO I see most days I'm out here.

'I told them you were the best busker in town and it would be a shame if they got rid of you. I hope it carries some weight,' he says. What a nice man!

A woman comes up after La Vie En Rose – I play this a few times today – twice I play it and twice people come up to request it again, which is rare. The woman tells me she likes all the old 50s Rock and Roll singers – Chuck Berry, Jerry Lee Lewis –

'He had a hard time when he came over here, though,' she says, referring to his marriage to his thirteen-year-old cousin.

'Yeah and they're still alive – most of them. Buddy Holly's dead, of course,' I say.

'Yes, it's funny how a lot of them die in plane crashes,' she says. Not really! '… and Little Richard, he's dead.'

'Is he? I'm sure he's still alive,' I say.

'He threw himself off a bridge, I thought – in Australia!'

'Did he – are you sure?'

'Or he threw some of his jewellery off it.'

Yes, I think that's probably more like it.

Near the end of my day a man pulls up in his motorised buggy and hands me a pound coin.

'Now, what are you going to play for me – play anything you like, anything you want.'

I thank him very much and ask if he knows some titles I do. I don't think he does.

'Oh you just play whatever you want.'

He's got a friendly face, this old man and I'm guessing he's not more than seventy-five at the most. I'm way off. His name is Henry Gray – 'that's G-R-A-Y' he says, '… and I'm ninety-nine.' Wow. I think he must be the oldest person I've ever met.

I tell him he looks a lot younger.

'Yes, many people say that,' he says and he takes off his cap and pats his head of slightly wavy white hair. He's got more hair and fewer wrinkles around the eyes than I have!

'Yes, I can remember all the songs we used to sing when we were children, from a hundred years ago – all the words, and someone from the village I lived in, near Oxford – Islip it was called, came down with a tape recorder and recorded me singing the songs. I remember all of them.'

'Really? And you live here now?'

'Yes, since 1960, but I've lived all over… the village where I lived – Islip, had a coat of arms of a man falling off a tree – I – slip, you see?'

Henry now lives in a home and has a man come in with a hot water bottle every morning. He needs one, even in the warm weather. 'They're very good there.'

So, what am I going to play for him? Only the song of the day – La Vie En Rose. I play it, looking down at my guitar, concentrating, not 'unhappy'. After a minute I look up and see Henry smiling and humming along, very quietly. He's ninety-nine years old and he's smiling and humming along – that's what I'm here for!

I chat to Simon the Big Issue seller who prefers to busk in the evenings.

'I don't like it in the day with all the people about, it's different at night but I get them all coming out of the pubs shouting "Play Wonderwall!" and it's so easy and boring. But if they shout some song out I don't know, I just say "You sing it, and I'll play it," and I can usually pick it up with a few chords and they're happy, you know – or I play little bits of things, like the Pink Panther one – do do, do do, do do… .'

The night shift, eh? He's a braver man than me.

Earnings: £37.69

DAY 86

Saturday April 23rd 2011
Winchester High Street, corner of Marks & Spencer
Time: 12:17-3:44pm

A hot day and yet the omnipresent stage jacket shall not be shed. Fortunately there is a breeze – a light one but just enough to disperse the heat somewhat. After an hour a lady comes up and asks if I would like a cold drink, presumably from the ice-lolly kiosk which has suddenly appeared across the pavement. I say thanks but no thanks as I'll have my small plum soon – one of the bunch given to me by Maurice the other day. I again dare to attempt my newest recruit to the set – Vincent, and make a few mistakes. I also have to stop for a few seconds to turn the page, having not memorised it yet, but this is getting embarrassing as page three is on the reverse of page two. I can see I'm going to have to

Henry Gray

separate them all. Even so, a woman gives me a pound but I apologise –

'Sorry, I haven't got that quite right yet!'

She says she's a singer so knows all about making mistakes in public – 'you just have to carry on, don't you?'

'Yeah. At least you know it'll be all over in a few minutes, I suppose.'

A little while later another lady comes up after I've made another mistake in a song. I apologise to her as well. She tells me that when she took piano lessons, if she played a wrong note, it would hurt. I was thinking she may have meant she got a rap on the knuckles from her teacher – she was about sixty so she might have been taking lessons fifty years ago, and piano teachers may have been able to get away with that sort of corporal musical punishment back then. Anyway, I'm curious –

'It hurt?'

'Yes. The vibrations that a wrong note causes would hurt me because they were the wrong vibrations!'

Very interesting. I've never heard anyone say that before. If that were the case for everyone, quite a few people I've played with would have passed out with the pain years ago. Come to think of it, after my attempt at Vincent, I'd be none too comfortable myself.

My banjo-less regular arrives on the scene – 'I still won't be playing the banjo for a while,' he says, looking at his be-slinged arm. I think he was knocked down while he was crossing the road recently. I believe he may have been in a state of quite severe intoxication.

I remind him of his party in July for which he wanted me to play – for a not unsubstantial amount. Is he still having his party?

'I'll keep you informed.'

Hmm. He takes up a semi-permanent position just to my right. In fact, he has plopped a £5 note in my bucket and so is entitled to a few requests – and to stay for awhile. So, any requests?

'I would really like to hear Harry Lime.'

Right you are, my good man. I play Harry Lime, aka The Theme From The Third Man… or just The Third Man. He, my requester, claps. Anything else, I ask.

'No, you just play what you want, I'll just listen.'

Good man. I believe I shall continue with… La Vie En Rose – I always think they go well together – that and TTM – same era, same guitar arranger, same key even.

While I'm playing, I notice a tall man wearing a baseball cap standing nearby and taking a photo, although he's taking his time with it. For a minute I think this is the tall guy who walked by me the other day who complained that I was 'always playing the same song', but why would he be taking a photo of me? To give to the police? It's strange what goes through the mind. Anyway this man looks much cleaner than the brute from the other day. I dismiss this silly thought.

However, the odd time I get a camera pointing at me I find it quite distracting, so I sometimes keep my head down to take my mind off it. When I look a minute later he's still there, taking the picture... but wait – I notice his camera has a black fuzzy thing attached to it – a microphone? Is this a video camera perhaps? I finish the tune and he comes up and asks me if I mind him putting me on his YouTube site – he gives me his card. His name's John and his site is called Daft Not Stupid. No, of course I wouldn't mind, but then I think – I made a couple of mistakes (ouch, ouch) in that song, I really should do another one – maybe The Third Man? After all I've just played it not more than ten minutes ago – I'm well rehearsed!

'Sure, you play it!' says John.

So be it and the performance is certainly better, although I *still* manage to fluff a note at the end. Pride comes... Whilst John is filming me, my seventy-three-year-old regular, Mabel, is walking towards me. I'm sure she's going to start talking to me – please Mabel, not now! However she sees the man with the camera and instead walks up past him, on film, puts some change in the bucket, smiles and walks off. After she walks away I'm thinking – has she cleaned my handkerchief I loaned her after she decided to clean all the street grilles with her bare fingers?

Before I pack up, my always smartly dressed regular – 'I'll have to become a tax exile, you're draining me of all my money!' – who I usually see up the other end of the road comes by. He's dressed more casually today but still smart in beige slacks and light blue casual shirt.

'You know, I like a man who can dress casually but still look smart,' I say.

'Oh yes, thank you,' he says, then apologises – 'I'm afraid I have nothing to give you today but my admiration!' Smooth.

Earnings: £34.25

DAY 87   Tuesday April 26th 2011
            Winchester High Street
            1. **Corner of Marks & Spencer. Time: 1:35-3:50pm**
            2. **Opposite Clinton Cards. Time: 4:21-6:08pm**

Three days of no busking (buskless?) seems like a long time these days and it took a while to get back in the swing, as it were. The weather was agreeable – not too warm with a breeze and I was able to play non-stop, apart from the half hour break between pitches. Even so, I still have a few problems, some easier to solve than others. The newest set recruit – Vincent, isn't coming along too well and there are a couple of times where my mind goes blank and I forget what comes next in some parts of other songs, like during a particular section of Barrios' Choro de Saudade, a piece I can play reasonably well at home but which often falls apart out here. When this happens, I immediately stop and go into something else – another song. I think this memory blank might be due to nerves – being self-conscious. I'm also having problems with Wheels, where I need to use three fingers of my right hand but I only have two that work. In other words, my focal dystonia is proving detrimental to the correct execution of this piece! The nerves I can solve by just a bit more practice, the focal dystonia is another thing…

My regular, George, turns up. He says he's got my music for Ave Maria in his car and he'll go and get it. He said he'd go and get it two weeks ago but he went and never came back! This time he does come back.

'Are you going to be here tomorrow?' he says.

I say I will, especially if it doesn't go well today.

'Oh good, I'm going to bring someone to see you – someone who you'll recognise.' Someone I'll recognise, eh? Someone famous, George? He won't say. I'm intrigued and decide to be here, at this place, at this time if today goes well or not.

Later, a man in his sixties who I've spoken to a couple of times – not enough for me to be honour him with the title of 'regular'! – stops to give me some shrapnel – 1 and 2p coins. He talks about a version of House of the Rising Sun by an orchestra in 1947 – no singing. I say I'd like to know the name of the orchestra but he can't remember. I ask him what he thought of The Animals version from '64. He thought it was great. And what about Dylan's version on his first album – that's where The Animals heard it. He doesn't answer but says he doesn't like 'some of these modern singers – they take some of the old songs and mess them up.' Indeed they do, my good man.

I finish up here. I haven't done too well – about thirteen pounds for over two hours' playing. I go over to Bertie before I head on up the road. He's curious – 'So, what's that style you play? I'm not being funny (that makes a change) but it sounds like you do two different songs at once – two melodies, with the bass thing… what's that called?' I explain the Merle Travis fingerstyle technique which evolved from Ragtime piano – the palm-muted bass part, the mid register chordal stabs, the higher register melody – all played with different fingers. This naturally leads me on to my describing my two useless fingers.

'So you'd be a lot better if they worked?'

'Yeah, I would!'

Bertie's sister plays a lot of Spanish/classical guitar.

'Ah, that's how you know to whistle to some of the ones I do!'

'Yeah,' he says, 'she's really good. She should come out here, I say to her.' I agree, she should. After my toilet break, I go to the cathedral grounds, eat my small orange then head back to the high street and set up halfway down the covered stretch.

A regular whose name – Mick, I find out today, chats to me about work on cruise ships.

'It pays well, I hear,' he says. Yes it does – but being stuck on a boat for a week and sharing a small cabin with some other boring middle-aged musician, well, I'm too old for all that now! Mick informs me of the best time to buy discounted food at Waitrose – six o'clock.

'What day, Mick?'

'Every day. Yesterday I got some prawns for…'

I like Mick, with his permanent cheeky smile. He's also got a habit several of my other regulars of a certain age seem to have – standing just behind and to the side of me and whistling along to whatever I'm playing before presenting themselves. Mick's also a musician which doesn't surprise me – Mick being a good name for a musician… of a certain age.

Later on, it's ninety-nine year-old Henry Gray but he doesn't stop on his way up the high street. He's bombing up at four miles per hour in his motorised buggy. 'Hello Henry!' I shout. He smiles. Goodbye Henry, soon to be one hundred.

Money-wise, it's been an OK day – £33 (well, almost) for four and a half hours. I've had worse and five minutes before I stop a young Chinese man puts a £5 note in the bucket.

Earnings: £32.99

Mick

DAY 88 **Wednesday April 27th 2011**
Winchester High Street
1. Opposite Marks & Spencer. Time: 1:01-1:45pm
2. Opposite Clarks. Time: 2:00-5:05pm

It's Market Day and no space for me at the usual place due to the fruit and veg stalls which crowd the area but Bertie persuades me to set up near him, on his side and 'see how it goes.' After I set up I think maybe I ought to have asked the fruit and veg seller who's a few feet away if he minds me being there. I go over –

'Makes no difference to me, mate – just don't play too loud,' he says.

'OK, you let me know if I do.' Doesn't he know I'm the quietest, most unobtrusive busker in town?

I play… and it doesn't go well – I've got just over £2 after three quarters of an hour so I decide to leave. Besides, the F & V guy is getting on my nerves with his relentless shouting of 'APARAGUS!' What's all that about – can't he pronounce S's if they're at the beginnings of words? I finish up with Jesu, Joy of Man's Desiring… and start it up again up the road fifteen minutes later.

I play As Time Goes By and get a virtual torrent of coins – two or more, in other words, so I play it three more times. A man walks by:

'All you need now is Judi Dench.'

I don't understand. He explains –

'Judi Dench – she was in that series – As Time Goes By.'

'Oh, right.'

Five minutes later he comes back while I'm playing La Vie En Rose and says 'Now you need Piaf!'

'Yeah, I've got more chance of seeing that Judi Dench walk by, I think.'

Later on, I've stopped to write something down and one of my regulars comes up, sees me writing, says he hopes he hasn't broken my train of thought then tells me of a famous poet, Kubla Khan – he thinks, who was in the middle of writing something of earth-shattering importance, was interrupted and never got it back.

'… so this is the stuff that gets written down – what's going on in your life at the moment, is it?' Yes, now please give me some money because I have noticed that you have stopped your contributions these last few weeks!

An old lady in her motorised buggy is heading straight for me… she stops right in front.

'Hee, Hee! He's always playing it – The Third Man!' she says to me.

If she's complaining, she's doing it with good nature, unlike the guy recently who I lost my temper with after his 'don't you know anything else?' remark. For him I had no patience, for this chuckling old lady I say 'It's the only song I know!' as she bombs off, still chuckling.

After two hours I haven't made much more than ten pounds and I'm getting cold – there's a strong wind and it's getting colder. I'm thinking it's been a bit of a waste of time coming out today when a man who looks like Jerry Garcia, the late Grateful Dead main man, puts a £5 note in the bucket and suddenly I can play a bit longer! Then I'm wondering about George from yesterday and the person he was going to bring along today who I would recognise. I've been here almost four hours and he hasn't turned up... but, there's a man who I see every time I'm out here – tall, bald and always wearing the same tatty multicoloured jumper and always carrying the same Harry Potter DVD which he holds out in front of him to look at for a second, as if he's consulting a map of the high street. He's always in a hurry. I'm reminded of these ghosts you read about – forever trapped in a particular place and time, always re-enacting some oft-played action from when they were flesh and blood, oblivious to all else and to our world. Very strange. The next time I see him, I must remember to grab the nearest person and ask them if he really is there...

Earnings: £33.30

DAY 89   **Friday April 29th 2011**
               Winchester High Street, corner of Marks & Spencer
               Time: 4:47-6:40pm

Royal Wedding or not, there's busking to be done and by late afternoon there should be some people about the town – well, that's what Alan, my friendly 75 years young street cleaner said when I saw him in a supermarket earlier. I'm reckoning many will have had a drink, or ten, so maybe there'll be a few in a more friendly, nay, even generous state of mind than usual. So, into town I go and yes, there are a few people around, not nearly as many as on a normal weekday but it'll do – and in my experience, the few people that *are* about are more giving of their attention.

THE FIRST HUNDRED DAYS

A few songs in, four teenagers – two boys and two girls walk by. One says 'those two hate the wedding!' pointing at 'those two'. As they turn the corner they give me the sign of Dionysius – forefinger and little finger outstretched, the two middle ones curled against the palm. This sign of the two-horned Greek god of pleasure is usually used by members of hard rock groups and their followers, not usually by tipsy teenagers. They disappear but come back a few minutes later to talk to me. They're quite cheerful and the blonde girl has definitely had one or two or three… or the aforementioned ten – 'Hey, are you Irish?'

'No, I lived in Canada for a long time. Have you been to a pub?'

'Naw, friend's house!'

'Oh, and you've had a couple of drinks?' I say, and nod towards the blonde.

'Yeah! What do you play – can you play Freebird?'

I get asked this often – why? – it's nothing like anything I play!

'No, sorry. Have a look at this set list.' I hand it to them and they all have a look.

'Mr. Sandman, yeah, can you play that?' says the blonde '… only I haven't got any money, look,' she says as she feels her skirt which hasn't got any pockets.

'It's OK,' I say and start playing. They walk off straight away, the blonde turning around to blow me a kiss – she really *has* had a few.

My next visitor is a young boy who comes and sits in front of me. He has a sweet face, blond hair and wears a small, black hat which looks like it's made of plastic. I finish the song and ask him if he plays the guitar. Yes he does – the classical guitar.

'Really? And do you have an acoustic guitar?'

'Yeah, I like yours though.'

'Thanks. I play a lot of Chet Atkins stuff, have you heard of him – he's an American guitarist, died about ten years ago.'

'Um… no, I'm nine years old (that's no excuse) so… no, that was before I was born.'

'Oh yeah, you're right. What's your name?'

'Ben. Do you need a license to play here?'

'Oh no, not in Winchester, you can just turn up anywhere here and play.'

'Oh, right, 'cause I dance!'

'Really? Well, yes, you can come here and dance if you like – make some money!'

He seems pleased by this and says, 'OK, thanks – you play great!' and goes off to join his parents on the bench, nearby.

One of my regulars turns up – the old man who lives in the St. Johns Almshouses down the road beyond the King Alfred statue. He wants to learn the guitar and I gave him my number months ago but he hasn't called to arrange a lesson. He's very curious and leans in close and asks me lots of questions about my guitar –

'… and what notes are those?' He points to a string. 'Are they the same as on the piano – C, D and so forth?'

'Well, yes and no – the open strings are E – that's the low one.'

'Which one's that?'

'The thickest one, here…' I put my finger on it.

'Yes, and the next one, what's that?'

'That's the A string, the A note.' I go through the whole lot – he asks me about every one. For once, I'm relieved I'm not playing one of my 12-string guitars!

He points to my thumbpick – 'And what is that, what does that do?'

'I use it to strike the notes, with this hand – my right hand.'

'And the other hand, what does that do?'

'My left hand? That one frets the notes.'

'Frets? What's that?'

'Frets? These are the frets' – I point to one. 'When I press down on the fret, it makes a note…'

'And how do the two hands correspond to each other? What is the relationship – do they do the same thing?'

'No. When I press the string–'

He interrupts – 'String? What's that?'

'What's what?'

'What did you call it?'

'A string? What's a STRING, you mean?'

'Yes.'

'A string, it's this thing here, this wire.'

'Yes, I see… and what does that do…'

Oh my goodness – this is going to take ages! What's a string?!

While I'm playing Jesu, Joy of Man's Desiring, another old man regular comes up. He listens then says 'They have a wedding and shut the world down! Anyway, you play well – who wrote that?'

'Thank you – a man called Johann Sebastian Bach.'

'Ah yes, Bach.'

'Yeah, he wrote it about three hundred years ago, something like that – it's a beautiful melody, isn't it?'

'Oh yes – here's a pound for you, please carry on.'

He walks off around the corner. I resume playing it and when I finish, he reappears – he must have been listening around the corner, out of sight! He again compliments me.

'Yes, very good – you play well.'

'Thank you very much, you're very kind!' I say, and he walks off again. I feel a bit sorry for him, his clothes are ill-fitting and could use a good clean.

So far, I'm pleased with the money that people are giving and, as I was predicting and hoping, the percentage of passers by who are contributing is definitely more than when there are many more about… a rough looking guy on a bike stops next to me and says in a quiet voice 'Do you smoke weed?'

'Me? No.'

'I've got two joints here, I want to sell 'em.'

'Hmm… sorry – no thanks!'

It's near the end – all in all, a pleasant day. I play Ol' Man River then La Vie En Rose – I've played it a few times today. People like it and it's one of the easier ones I do. Four people a bit older than me walk by. One of them – a man, breaks off from his companions and comes over. He waits until I've stopped playing before he speaks – very polite. I wish more would do this instead of coming over and talking straight away, over the music!

'That Chet Atkins has a lot to answer for!' He's a Scotsman (or someone putting on a Scottish accent).

'Ah you guessed the arrangement!'

'Oh yes, I could hear him in that.'

'I do a lot of his arrangements – Ol' Man River – the other one you heard, that's one of his, on the CD of stuff he recorded at home which wasn't released till after he died.'

'Really? I got the first album he made – Chet Atkins' Workshop in 1962.'

He is mistaken! Chet's first album was made in 1954.

'Yes, I've got that one, too,' I say, keeping silent about his gross inaccuracy.

'I had some friends who actually met him, *and* played with him, in Tennessee – where did he live?'

'Nashville.'

'Yes, Nashville! They were all good musicians – your calibre (you're too kind, my man) and after they were playing, Chet Atkins said "Hey, you guys are better than me!"'

'Wow!' I say. 'Mind you, I've read he was quite a humble guy, so I can believe he said that.'

'Anyway, you take care, and thank you – that's brightened up my day.' And with that, he walks off to join his friends who are unlocking their bicycles on the other side of the road. A nice man to bring to a close this late, not too gruelling (almost pleasant, even) session resulting in £23 in just under two hours.

Earnings: £23.26

DAY 90   Saturday April 30th 2011
               Bath city centre, outside The Pump Room
               Time: 6:42-7:55pm

A new location in a new town and on approaching the city centre I'm a bit nervous, as I am before busking in any place I haven't played before. I'm also hungry – I eat my small apple, walking down Gay Street. It's quite a late one for me – almost seven o'clock and in Winchester there wouldn't be many about, but there are hundreds of pubs and restaurants down here and a lot of people about. On other (non-playing) visits, I've always noticed someone playing near the Abbey where there are a few benches around a small square, so I head there and, yes – there is someone there, playing a guitar to a backing track. So I walk past this guy and around the square… down a little street and come up outside the Pump Room(s). I remember I played at a wedding here a few years ago, in a loud covers or 'cabaret' group, as I call them. Back then, I was inside, now I'm on the other side!

I set up against the wall – there's a bench nearby with a couple of women on it. I start my Bath debut with La Vie En Rose and get a few coins from two Chinese people walking by. In fact most of the people walking by seem to be Chinese! – something else I recall from before. Two young guys, one with a guitar, give me some money. I thank them and ask if they are going to do some busking now. No they're not – they've done their four hours a week, they only do a day. I ask them what it's like here – in other words, I'm trying to find out how much they make! After a few minutes of my probing, they say they get 'maybe thirty pounds an hour.' That's really good, I say. I ask their names – Taro, or Taron, and Mat – 'with one T'. They tell me of when they went busking in the blizzard and did very well, there being no other buskers about. Sympathy money! – like when I did my first day in Southampton and the lady who gave me a pound 'for perseverance in the rain' – an utterance I'll probably never forget. We say goodbye and they head off around the corner towards the Abbey.

Later, three young men walk by. One says, 'You're better than me!' I say thanks, then think – I'm assuming he's another musician but he might be a butcher or work in a shoe shop! Still, it's a scarcely heard remark. Another group of young guys walk by, one puts some coins in the bucket. I say thanks and he turns around and says 'It's only 3p, sorry – it's all I've got.' That's honest – he didn't have to admit it was only 3p.

'It's okay, thanks anyway,' I say.

Then they stop a bit further on and one of the others gets something out of '3p's' rucksack. 3p comes back to me – it's a can of Scrumpy Jack cider and he plonks it in my bucket.

'That's my cider, now you've got that and my 3p!'

I thank him again and carry on playing but now I look like a tramp with a can of strong cider poking out of my bucket. Even so, I wait five minutes before I take it out and hide it behind my amplifier, which isn't much bigger than the can.

My last acquaintance during my Bath debut is a man who stops to listen across the road for a few minutes… then sits down on the bench and listens for a few more minutes – he's obviously in no rush to get anywhere. After I finish The Entertainer, he claps and says:

'That was done by some old blues guy, wasn't it?'

I tell him Scott Joplin wrote it, for the piano.

'Yes, I know, but didn't some blues guy, someone like Robert Johnson do it?'

I don't think so, I say.

This man knows I'm an outsider (an outsider in cider!) – 'I haven't seen you here before,' he says.

'No, I usually play in Winchester, I'm just here for a day or so. I'll be here tomorrow – if I can get a place for a couple of hours, that is.'

This man thinks all the buskers meet up near the Abbey in the morning to work out their times of playing. I'll have to take my chances, then. Anyway, my acquaintance really thinks I should be playing this stuff in Browns, a local eatery. He gives me the golden compliment, the ultimate accolade – I've brightened up his day and made him smile. But it's time I was away – I have a pressing dinner engagement at an establishment in five minutes time… and it's twenty minutes walk away. I pack up while my admirer tells me all about his problems with his teeth and the titanium implants the hospital are going to put in them. I've made just over eleven pounds for just over an hour, an acceptable rate for my Bath debut. Yes, a pleasant hour – the only annoyance being a posh man who interrupted me mid-song to ask the way to Bath Springs (?) Like many posh people, he has more money than manners.

Earnings: £11.42 + 1 can of Scrumpy Jack cider

DAY 91   **Sunday May 1st 2011**
            Bath city centre, doorway of Topman, opposite Cult
            Time: 11:55-1:50pm

Once again I stroll down from the hills – where all the people live, to the city centre – where all the people go, and unlike last night, there are a few other buskers about. There's someone setting up a small drum kit in the open space near the Abbey… and a young lady strumming an acoustic guitar at the same place I made my Bath debut last night, in front of the Pump Room.

'Hello there, how's it going?' I ask politely, even though she's taken my place! She says it's OK, she's collecting for charity – 'I've got about four pounds.' Indeed, she's got a hand written note which actually says FOR CHARITY, which I suppose could be her name. I ask her how long she's been here. Twenty minutes.

'OK, good luck,' I say. On the other side of the street are two young strummers – a boy and girl, who I can't hear – there's so much noise and hundreds, nay thousands of people.

So, where to go… I carry on walking, down towards the train station… back again… and they're all still there… down the road again – here's an unused doorway and the shop, a Topman or Topshop, looks like it's closed down. There's a café across the way and down a bit, and a few benches in the middle – it's a pedestrian road, like a lot of this area of Bath. I set up, sit down and look at the pavement around me, covered with pigeon droppings! To hell with it. I start playing, the weather's fine – not too warm, or cold and there's a pleasant breeze.

A fellow Chet Atkins fan gives me some money after La Vie En Rose. I tell him the arrangement is from a CD of home recordings Chet did but which weren't released until after he died. I inform him that I do another one – Ol' Man River from the same album. 'Do you? Could you play that one?' Yes, of course. He likes it, then his wife and child show up and drag him off.

I play The James Bond Theme a couple of times. I've noticed people are often surprised to hear this, particularly after something like Mr. Sandman or As Time Goes By. It's good to do something unexpected – people will suddenly look up from a book or a paper. During Music To Watch Girls By, I suffer another memory blank and fumble around with a few bars of mainly wrong notes then give up. Oh dear.

My time here is almost done when two Polish men turn up. They love my sound but can one of them play a song of his on my guitar? OK, it's near the end – I've had a good session and one guy even gave me a £5 note – that always makes my day.

The Polish man says he's a singer, and yes, he would love to borrow my guitar to play his song. He plays and sings with great gusto throughout. I haven't quite got the Polish dialect under my belt and have no idea what is going on in this song, apart from it's about four minutes long. When he finishes, his friend says that now *he* would like to have a play. OK, but just one minute I say and hold up one finger just to make sure they get my drift. OK, he says. As he's playing, I ask the first guy his name and also the name of his song. His name is Greg (which doesn't sound very Polish to me) and his song's called We Give Our Heart To Poland, so now I know why he was singing so passionately! And he is very passionate about his song. And his country – 'I say to you, I will give my blood (he pounds his chest)… for my country! I will give my heart!' Admirable, although hopefully he won't have to do that, unlike a lot of his fellow countrymen in the past.

Greg also plays the keyboards and wants to form a band with me. But there's a problem, geography-wise. I tell them I don't live in Bath, I live in a far distant land called Winchester.

'How far is that?' he asks.

'About forty English country miles,' I say. But I don't really want to be in a group with him, anyway. Not really. So… thank you for your spare change and offer of recruitment, Greg, but anyway, it's time for me to say goodbye – to my two new Polish friends and also to Bath, with its hectic city centre and fine Georgian buildings and crescents. Who knows, I may return one day...

Earnings: £24.07

DAY 92

Friday May 6th 2011
Winchester High Street, corner of Marks & Spencer
Time: 5:03-6:27pm

I'm in a bad mood today and will be for the next three weeks or the foreseeable future, whichever comes first. I have lost one of my hearing aids, the one I put behind my left ear and it will take my ever efficient local hospital – the Royal Hampshire County Hospital, three weeks to get me a new one, at a cost of £65. I'm not the only one in a bad mood – Simon, the usually friendly, chatty, night shift busker/Big Issue seller also seems to be in one. I pass him near the HMV Shop as he is talking to a beggar who's sitting down. Two minutes later, I've put my two bags down and I'm about to set up when Simon walks by and, not looking at me, mutters 'Some people take the piss.'

I'm not sure if it's directed at me – maybe he thinks I've taken his pitch, although in my experience if someone is going to buy a Big Issue, they'll do it if there's a busker nearby or not and conversely, if someone wants to give a busker a pound, they'll do it whether or not there's a guy selling a magazine. But I don't like someone walking by saying something like that. I wait a minute then go over to him. He's sitting down in front of Sainsbury's with his Big Issues, looking miserable. I don't blame him. I'd be miserable sitting down there trying to sell a magazine.

'You OK? I'm not taking your spot, am I?'

'No, it's OK,' he says.

I'm not convinced.

'I don't mind going up the road, outside Smiths.'

'Naw, it's nothing, that other guy's there anyway.' He means the tramp he was talking to. '... it's not you, you carry on, mate.'

'You sure?'

'Yeah, you carry on – it's nothing to do with you, you carry on, mate.'

'Right, well OK, I'm only going to do an hour, but you tell me if it's me though.' He really is down, he usually talks to/at me for at least twenty minutes.

Oh well. I set up and play and immediately feel uncomfortable – my amplifier is on my left side and without my hearing aid, the sound is quiet and muffled. I'm not used to it, it's all wrong! I'll have to put the amp on my right side, either that or turn around and face the wall, with my back to my adoring audience but with my sole hearing-aided ear nearest to the sound. Hmm… this will be difficult, for I am a man of habit and tradition. I will see how I get on today…

A few weeks ago I made the acquaintance of several actors/dancers who have Down's Syndrome. They were rehearsing a play up at the Tower Arts Centre. They sometimes come up and stand next to me for a few minutes. They do so today – as soon as I'm about to start, two appear from around the corner. Their play's debut performance is tomorrow and they're pretty confident about it all. I'll miss it as I'll be doing a hybrid gig/busking spot in London, but hope to see a later show. I saw a rehearsal, they're very good. One pats me on the head and gives me a penny.

I am visited by the friendly old man who lives at the nearby almshouses. He's holding a tissue covered in blood up to his nose.

'Oh dear, a nose bleed?' I say.

'Yes, I do get them. I like what you play. Do you learn each song at a time?'

'Um… yes, but sometimes I'll be learning three or four at once, depending on how difficult some of them are. Some of them I've been learning for years! But at the same time I can work on other ones that don't take as long.' I ask him if he has a guitar yet. He doesn't but was looking at one the other day for £250. I say he doesn't need to spend that much – he could get one at a car boot fair for next to nothing. I tell him he doesn't need one like this one I've got.

'No… do you think you could look for one for me?' He's said this a couple of times before.

'Yeah OK, I'll look out for one.'

'Anyway,' he says, 'I like Spanish music – that Aran… something.'

'Ah, the Concierto de Aranjuez you mean? By Rodrigo.'

'Yes, do you play it?'

'Me? Oh no – that's for the orchestra and guitar, isn't it? No, I only do the easier ones, I'm afraid!'

My regular, the quite friendly, often generous and occasionally quite drunk one who keeps threatening to bring along his banjo for me to tune, shows up. He's just bought a frying pan, which he shows to me, holding it like a banjo. 'Will you be here next week?' he says (my world is full of old men who keep repeating themselves) … I'll bring it along.'

'Yeah, I'll be around, I see your arm's better.' He was run over or something but no longer has his sling.

'Yes, it's amazing how fast it's healed. Now, I wonder if you could play Harry Lime for me,' he says as he puts a five pound note in my bucket. This turns out to be half the total amount I make today in the 1½ hours I'm out here.

'I sure can!' I play and because, by now, I can play it backwards and with my eyes shut, I can also talk to him at the same time.

'I really do love that – I wonder why,' he says… and wonders.

'Because it's simple – it's only three notes, next to each other!' I offer, as an explanation as good as any other.

Earnings: £10.14

DAY 93   Saturday May 7th 2011
            Ladbroke Grove, London, outside The Elgin public house
            Time: 1:00-5:45pm

A curious one, this – something of a hybrid in that it's a combination of a 'proper' gig, for which I received payment! – unusual in London, I have to say, to the eternal shame of 99% of landlords – and a busking session. The pub, The Elgin, is run by an old acquaintance, Robin Smith, who was one of a band of Scouse musicians terrorising south London twenty years ago, the same time I was living there. Hmm… I ruminate on how fate is a strange thing – Robin now runs a popular pub on the busy and ever trendy Portobello Road while I busk on street corners. Hmm… So from one to four o'clock in the afternoon, I am 'contracted' to perform an informal set at one end of a rectangular area at the side of the pub. At the other end there is a guy roasting sausages and hamburgers – in short, it's a barbecue. Mr. Smith says it's also okay for me to put my collection bucket in front of me, which is good as I'm hoping to cover the train fare and not dig into my contracted fee for this.

Because I'm not sure how loud I'll have to be – but I'm pretty sure Portobello Road is louder than Winchester High Street, I take my bigger busking amp and also no less than two guitars – my usual trusty 6-string electric busking guitar and also my lovely 12-string acoustic which I use for doing my own songs. I might do some of them, I'm not sure yet.

I leave my house in the morning and three trains later, I'm at Ladbroke Grove – a part of London I haven't been to for twenty years, apart from when I saw Duck Baker at a tiny club a few years ago. But I remember those olden days – when I was still pretty young. I used to cycle all around London. I had a weird sort of ghoulish interest in some of the post-war London murderers, in particular John Christie, the necrophiliac who lived in Rillington Place, just around the corner from Ladbroke Grove underground station. He buried the bodies in his back yard and in the wall cavities in his house. The police got him in 1953 but not before they hanged an innocent man, Timothy Evans, in one of the most infamous miscarriages of justice. Ludovic Kennedy wrote a book about it and there was a film made in the actual house in the actual street before they tore it all down, rebuilt it and changed the name – to Bartle Road, I think. I remember I was really fascinated by all that! Why do young people get obsessed by weird criminals?! In fact, if I remember, The Elgin was one of the pubs that Timothy Evans used to drink in. The other was the Kensington Park Hotel, or the KPH, I think he called it… anyway, it looks like the police are here again. They've sealed off a road I need to cross to get to the pub which means I have to walk around the block. I think I'm going in the right direction but still ask the way, to make sure. I ask eight people – not one knows, as they are all from somewhere else in the world. There are thousands of people about and much, much noise – it's Portobello Road and it's Saturday afternoon! There's a small steel band combo outside one pub.

I finally get to my destination – The Elgin, and greet my benefactor/employer for the afternoon, Mr. Smith. I dump my bags which were getting heavier and heavier and cool down with a glass of Coca-Cola – on the house! … and after a quick think and a consultation with Mr. Smith, I decide it's probably better to stick with the well-known 'crowd pleasers', and ditch my own songs as I'm none too sure a nine minute song about a balloon and another about visiting a funeral home to view the corpse of a childhood sweetheart are appropriate for a sunny afternoon's barbecue. But why the police presence? Mr. Smith tells me there's been a bomb scare, which doesn't surprise me, as the Yanks – our allies, have just killed that bad Arab man, Mr. Bin Laden. Bomb scares in London used to be linked to the IRA – I remember playing in a restaurant in London Bridge around 1993 with my old mate Paul, when they blew up a car which was parked just outside. I suppose it's someone else's turn now.

On to the music… I set up and start with La Vie En Rose, after which a couple of people clap. I play the Third Man, after which one person claps. My benefactor, who is sitting with his two children who have just finished their burgers, leaves. I think he just wanted to make sure I wasn't rubbish! I find out later his children don't like my music – I don't blame them, I was in my thirties before I got into fingerstyle stuff and Chet Atkins. I play for two hours straight through, the smoke from the barbecue blowing over me all the time. I don't mind this as it's quite a pleasant smell and this is all a welcome change from the usual – struggling to make a few quid in Winchester High Street. A young Polish guy gives me a five pound note! I'm certainly meeting my fair share of Poles this week, first Bath, now here. I get one of the oddest requests ever, even more bizarre than Freebird, it's a request for Metallica – Nothing Else Matters. No. I've never even heard it.

Just before three o'clock a French man wants 'any Beatles, I love Beatles!' and he gives me a TEN pound note! 'Sure Monsieur! Just let me find my capo' … it's gone, I haven't brought it or it's lost, I can't do the song… I find it! I *can* do the song! I play Here Comes The Sun. I decide to take a two minute break so I switch my amp off… .then when I switch it on again, the light goes on then off and won't go on again. I panic – what if my amp's gone? I have another hour to do. I open the battery compartment and there's all this liquid or acid or something on the batteries. I take them out with my fingers and a pen. Oh dear, I'll have to get some more so I tell the barbecue guy I'll be back soon.

The first newsagent doesn't stock batteries and the second doesn't have the right size – what's wrong with this place, this is one of the biggest cities in the world! But I get some from the third place I go to, near the tube station. I return and… the amp works. Good. I do another hour which takes me to ten past four, just over my contracted time although, in busking terms, I've just warmed up. I've had a pleasant time, the weather's been fine, I've managed to get sixteen pounds in the bucket and my own arrangement of The James Bond Theme went down well. I pack up and go into the bar where a gentleman of Rastafarian persuasion engages me in conversation. He's a musician himself (naturally), and just finished his bit somewhere else – I've a sneaking suspicion he's got something to do with the steel band combo, earlier. Where are the other buskers, he asks me. What's this? What does he mean? He points to a sign that says FREE COCKTAILS, BARBECUE AND BUSKERS. So it does, but no, it's just me today.

It's pay packet time! A friendly young Australian guy (naturally) hands me the cash, for which I thank him. 'No worries!' he says. It's good to be properly paid, I'm not used to it and it puts me in a benevolent frame of mind and a good mood, despite the loss of my hearing-aid which is a bit of a permanent small cloud over me at the moment. I ask No Worries if he would mind if I do another set – while I'm here!

'Yeah, you play as long as you want, mate! – can't pay you any more though.'

I say that's fine, I don't want anything else. So I unpack all my stuff, set up and do another set – after all, I'm well-rehearsed by now! ... this takes me to 5:45. I get another four quid in the bucket – good, that's sorted the train fare, like I was hoping. I pack up again and then I'm off, back to Waterloo, on the train with a bunch of shaven-headed, swearing, football fans – some of the men were quite boisterous, too.

I get back to Winchester at half past eight, my back done in – I'm too old to be carrying an electric guitar, a 12-string jumbo acoustic guitar and an amplifier all over the place. On arrival at home, Mr. Smith has left a phone message – maybe I can come up again? I hope to, it was a nice change. It's a shame I have to go to London to get paid decent money but no place in Winchester is interested – I've tried them all. I can't believe I can't get a gig in my 'home' town! Anyway, when I took my guitar out of the bag, all I could smell was the smoke from the barbecue.

Busking earnings: £20.00

DAY 94   **Monday May 9th 2011**
                 Winchester High Street
                 1. Opposite Clinton Cards. Time: 1:35-2:45pm
                 2. Corner of Marks & Spencer. Time: 2:50-6:05pm

I see Frank sitting on the bench outside WH Smiths, without accordion and also without dog.

'You not playing today, Frank?'

'No, just people watching. Colin (trumpeteering busker – always with a helpful tip for us less experienced buskers) is down at the other end, so you've got the street to yourself.'

I set up and play and it's twenty-five minutes before I get the first coin, from my Italian lady, Delia, who has been listening from just behind me – I know she's been there, I can just see her in the corner of my eye. She thinks I can't – I know! I stop playing.

'Oh, don't stop,' she says.

'Well, thank you, Delia – you're my first customer.' I ask about her ear problem. It's a bit better, she's got to put some olive oil in to clear it up. Yes, I know all about olive oil – the best thing, just ordinary olive oil, not the stuff they charge a fortune for in the chemist. I know all about it, I say, as I have a narrow ear canal in one of my ears…

A man compliments me on my As Time Goes By arrangement (though he still doesn't contribute to the 'cause') and reckons I should get it up on the internet, but I don't even regard it as a proper arrangement. Colin, the tipful trumpeteering busker walks by. He's finished down at the bottom. He's got guts – he sets up right in the middle of the street, whereas I set up against the wall of the shop. I wonder if he has any more helpful tips for me.

'Hi there,' he says and looks at my bucket. 'I've got a good tip (I knew it!)… what you do is you cut the top of your bucket right round and leave just a couple of inches on the bottom, then put the top back on. That way, if anyone tries to steal it they leave the bottom with all your money in. 'Cause it happened to me, it was terrible, y'know.'

'Hm… yeah, I see what you mean.'

'Yeah, and if they pick it up by the handle, they just lift the top off!'

'Yeah, well, I might try that.'

If anyone tried to rip me off right now they'd get away with £4.75, as this is what I've made in an hour and a half – not good so I'm going to move down where Colin's just been, not in the middle of the road, in my usual darkened spot.

It's better straight away – and in the sun, but not too warm, with a nice breeze. I'll park here for a bit. A man comes up and is convinced I am another busker who plays Bob Dylan and Fleetwood Mac songs.

No, that's not me, sorry (why apologise?)

But he's sure it *is* me – 'I'm one hundred per cent sure and I never forget a face.'

Well, they say there's a first time for everything and he's clearly forgotten the face of the guy who *does* play Bob Dylan and Fleetwood Mac because it's not mine – unless I have a double working here in the high street.

I see a man coming up the road on the other side of the street and I'm sure it's the Scottish bloke who went nuts when I played the Smoke On

The Water riff a while back. I'm finishing La Vie En Rose, he comes over and leans in – 'You ever been to Louisiana?'

'No.'

'Well, that's where all that music yer playin' is from – the blues. Never been to Georgia? Alabama?'

'Nope, never.'

'And yer playin' that music – blues? And you don't know it's from over there, the southern states?'

'What – La Vie En Rose?'

'What?'

'What I'm playing – La Vie En Rose. It's Edith Piaf, it's French!'

'Oh… well… I haven't got any pennies… hey, enjoy the sunshine!'

'Yeah, OK.'

Indeed, the sun is out and the song of the day is As Time Goes By. I've played it five times already and it's earned me a couple of pounds, at least.

A lady comes up – 'Were you on that talent show, Britain's Got Talent?'

'Me? No way!'

'I'm sure it was you. You play a guitar.'

No, I say again, it wasn't me – what is this, the day of mistaken identity or something?

She goes on – 'What was his name?… oh… Armstrong, yes! Someone Armstrong from Waterlooville, but they showed him playing in Winchester.'

'Right, well it was probably a younger guy, but my name's not Armstrong, it's Naylor!'

A familiar and strange character walks by – the man who walks with a purpose, always clutching the same Harry Potter DVD. But today he's got a tanned face and a rucksack on his back with one of those foam mats you roll out to make a bed with when you're camping – a so-called 'leisure' activity I avoid at all costs, but I've seen other people do it and they have these things they roll up and tie on to the top of their rucksacks.

A lady gives some change and says 'You should play in the Shetland Islands – you'd like it there, I've just been.'

'Yes, I bet it would be nice. Trouble is, who's going to pay my train fare?'

'Ha, yes… well, are you going to play Yellow Bird?'

'Yeah, OK. I played it an hour ago, it's about time I did it again – just let me change the tuning, I have to change two strings, y'see… I have to lower them… have you heard me play this before?'

'Yes, and it always reminds me of my mother.'

Interesting – I've heard this same thing from other ladies.

'OK, Yellow Bird, here you go…'

I have to admit I like playing this – it's a great Chet Atkins arrangement and not too tiring for my bad right hand and I can add as many verses and bridges I want as the separate melodies are all so memorable, so it never gets boring – not for me, anyway. A man in his sixties listening on the bench opposite comes over – 'I remember the songs, that's the trouble!' and laughs. And again I wonder what I'll do when all the people who know these old songs – and give money – all die off…

A couple of ladies with a pram talk to me and give me a notepad they've bought for a pound from the er… poundshop, around the corner. They ask if I'm 'going to do another article in the paper', to which I give my standard reply – 'it's not up to me but by all means, write to them and say you want to read more or better still, you can go to their office and tell them in person, it's just around the corner!'

They ignore me and move on – 'and here is Baby Elizabeth…'

Earnings: £36.28.

DAY 95   Thursday May 12th 2011
            Winchester High Street, opposite Vodafone
            Time: 1:58-4pm, 4:32-6pm

I've had a three-day break but now it's time to go back to 'work'. As I approach the Buttercross I notice a man wearing sunglasses, a hat and a blue boiler suit sitting down against the monument, a two wheel cart next to him. I don't recognise him but as I walk past, I hear 'Marvin' – it's Frank. He seems to be decked out in all different gear today and the cart looks like another one – much more colourful than the usual. I go over and apologise for not recognising him – it must be his summer look, with the shades. Frank asks if I've heard about the council's plans to introduce the buskers' permit. For an initial fee of ten pounds, the buskers will be allowed to perform – in certain spots. I've heard about this from Bertie, but until it happens it's just a rumour. Anyway, I'm not bothered about it – in fact it's supposed to clear the high street of the beggars because the police don't want to be bothered with asking them to move on – they have to let them stay if they suddenly produce a penny whistle, small drum, etc., and start 'playing'.

Which reminds me, I haven't seen the small drum beggar around recently. Frank tells me why. Apparently he's in jail for hitting his neighbour in the face with a big plank of wood after the neighbour complained about the loud music he was playing. Frank reckons he's going down for attempted murder, or GBH 'at the least'. He reckons we won't be seeing him for a while. Wait! – this was the same guy I lost my temper with a few months ago – who objected to me setting up near him. Cripes!

Two girls about twenty years old and carrying guitars walk by. Frank reckons they're looking for a spot and it's just this part of the high street that's buskable today – the market is all down the other end. It used to be just Wednesday, now it's Thursday and Friday as well. This sort of puts one of my favourite spots – the corner of Marks and Spencer, out of bounds, as it's too close to the stalls. The girls have walked down a bit and are now coming back. Frank advises me to go and get a spot before they do. I walk quickly and catch up with them just as they put their stuff down around the middle of the covered stretch. I suppose I could have overtaken them and got to the spot a few seconds earlier but that ain't no way to behave to a couple of young ladies! It's not the end of the world.

I say hello and ask if they're buskers.

'Yeah, did you want this place?'

'It's OK, I can go down there (there's a spot at the bottom near the jewellers).How long do you usually do?'

'About an hour, we think.'

'OK, good luck!'

I walk down the road to the spot – there's enough distance between us, they won't hear me. I start with La Vie En Rose – quite a habit these days.

Afterwards, a man comes up and puts a pound in the bucket – 'Now, what are you going to play me?'

'Thank you very much, this one…' The Third Man, naturally.

This man plonks himself down against the wall next to me. Don't get too comfortable, pal, I think to myself. He talks to me while I'm playing. His name's Dave, or 'Dangerous Dave, as they used to call me, but I've calmed down a bit. I'm fifty now, I can't carry on like that.' Good, I'm pleased he's calmed down. Hm… there *is* something scary, yes – even dangerous, about him – he has a hard looking face. I play the Theme from the Good, the Bad and the Ugly – Dangerous Dave likes themes.

'Yeah, that sounds like Apache, The Shadows, can you play that?'

'No, sorry Dave.'

He's not angry at me, which is good. He says goodbye and walks off. The two girls walk past, they only did forty minutes! You gotta stick with it out here, ladies!

I've got my head down and suddenly there's a finger almost touching one of my guitar strings.

'So that's the sixth string, is it?'

It's the old gentleman who wants to learn how to play the guitar.

'Oh hello, yes.'

Then, pointing to the first string – 'And that's the first, is it?'

'Yep, and that's the third, and that's the fourth…'

I go through them all. Then I ask how he's getting on with his guitar tuition books he bought from a charity shop.

'Well, there's a lot to go through, isn't there? I just want to make sure I know a bit so I'm not wasting your time' – he would like me to give him some lessons. The trouble is, he's trying to learn about the guitar but he hasn't got one – it's crazy! I feel a bit sorry for him – he doesn't look like he's got much money, maybe he can't afford even a cheap guitar. Hm… I have a quick think and have an idea. I say I'll bring a guitar for him – a small nylon string one I don't play. He can have it – 'you can't learn an instrument with just a book!' I say. So we agree to meet here the same time tomorrow, about three o'clock. I tell him that I'll definitely be here. Will *he*? He says he will…

A lady comes up and asks if I watched the DVD about the man and the jellyfish – stung by five box jellyfish, I think she said. I'm thinking about playing and – these people *will* come up and just start talking while I'm in the middle of playing something! And I don't know what she's on about.

Five Box Jellyfish? 'Is that a group or something?' I say.

'No!' – she sounds put out.

Then I remember – this is the Christian lady who gave me the DVD with the guy giving the talk about how he was stung by these deadly jellyfish and he died for twenty minutes then came back to life. I did play it but the picture froze up after an hour, just when he was getting to the crucial bit – in the hospital, just before he supposedly/allegedly died. I tell her this.

'Oh, the next bit is him saying why Jesus chose *him* to come back to life – are you a Christian?'

'No, I don't follow any religion. I still find this stuff interesting, though. Do you have another video I can try?'

Yes she does. I promise to watch the end bit…

'Legless' Brian, Maurice's friend, scoots by in his wheelchair – 'Hello Brian.'

No response – he never returns my greetings.

A young lady, one of a bunch of people who are wearing jackets with POVERTY written on the back – they've been around this area the whole time, comes up to me –

'Can I just say you're WICKED!'

'Thanks… is that good?'

'Yeah, wicked – awesome!'

'Well… OK, thanks. How are you getting on?'

She says she's got thirty-five signatures but needs to get at least fifty.

'What if you don't?'

'I get the sack!'

'Really?'

'No, probably not.'

She gets a lot of abuse, she says. It's one job I'm glad I'm not doing. This whole busking business gets pretty depressing sometimes, like when it's cold or when I've played for half an hour and not got a penny, but I wouldn't do *her* job. I tell her about *my* line – how I won't get anything for ages then suddenly loads of people will come up. It's like that with her job, too. I suppose it helps to have a cheerful disposition, which she seems to have. I ask her name. 'It's Emily, Emily Scott.'

I have another fan – the guy from the Nokia shop, opposite. He's been standing outside, handing out leaflets. He comes over to say he really likes my James Bond number – 'It's really cool.' The lady from the bakery is out in the street giving out very small pieces of something on a tray. She comes over to me – 'Would you like some pumpkin bread?' 'Yeah OK, it's about my snack time, anyway.' I get the last two bits, and they really *are* bits.

I take a break as I've been playing non-stop for two hours. So it's to the cathedral to eat my small apple… then back to set up three feet away from the other spot – for a small change of scenery. Frank's finished up the road and he comes by – 'I've just had two little girls running around the Buttercross on skateboards for the last hour. How do you tell 'em?'

'I don't know Frank, stick your foot out?'

Off he goes. Then, not five minutes later, there's a little girl with a skateboard in front of *me*! She starts dancing, then I hear a lady shout 'COME ON! Or we'll get a parking fine!' and the kid's gone. I've been spared.

I'm on the final stretch and there are six teenagers standing near me, just to my left. One comes up and pretends to pick my bucket up and walks back to the rest. I make sure they see my look of displeasure then, one by one, they all come up and put money in, mainly very low denomination coins – shrapnel. Still, I thank them. It turns out they're French – from Picardy, near Paris, and they're soon joined by about twenty more and their two adult guardians/teachers. They all stand in front of me and all the others start putting change in the bucket.

'When are you going back?' I say.

'Tomorrow,' says the lady guardian/teacher.

'Ah, and you need to get rid of your English coins?'

As par for the course when confronted by the French, I say I will play La Vie En Rose, although I'm sure none of the kids will know it.

'Ah, La Vie En Rose!' she says, turning to her bunch.

I play it and at the end they don't clap – unlike my more polite bunch from a few months ago, but one comes up and gives some change, followed by all the others – every other one! I say 'Merci' to them all, along with quite a few 'Au Revoir's, which is about all I can remember from the Holiday French course I did six years ago. I must have known a few other things – I still have the certificate they gave me... and everyone else.

Earnings: £37.25

DAY 96   Friday May 13th 2011
          Winchester High Street
          1. Opposite WH Smiths. Time: 1-2:20pm
          2. Opposite Vodafone. Time: 2:55-6:30pm

I open the session with a mellow (it's only ever that) As Time Goes By – a real money-spinner the other day. There's an elderly man with a walking stick standing just behind and to the left of me. They often stand where they think I can't see them, but I know they're there – always! I know the song became really well-known because of Casablanca, in 1942, but it had been around for ten years before that. After I play it, the man goes through the 'Play it again Sam!' routine, but Bogart never said it. He said (to Sam) – 'You played it for her, you can play it for me! Play it!' My man tells me that Bogart got his distinctive lispy thing from some accident he had when he was in the navy, when he was young. We talk further but I need to get playing – it's fifteen minutes in and I've only done one song.

I do The Third Man and he's still there at the end – the old man, not the third man.

'You need to get a Homburg – like Orson Welles, so you can put it on when you're doing that, or you could have a box with all different hats to wear, like Tommy Cooper in that sketch he did.'

'Oh yeah, I see what you mean.' I ponder this '... but it would be just another thing I'd have to carry around with me – a box full of hats.'

Today's Song Of The Day? Wheels – another great Chet Atkins arrangement. I have great trouble with parts of this due to my focal dystonia, so any compliment is greatly appreciated, especially if it takes the form of a five pound note, which it does today. The 'blue' note, as it were, is followed incredibly by four or five other donations, about a pound each. Yes, definitely SOTD.

Another old guy hovers in the background and waits until I've finished the song before he comes up.

'I cremated my wife – after sixty-eight years,' he says.

What, after sixty-eight years? This sounds a bit odd but I don't want to make light of whatever he means.

'Oh, did you? After sixty-eight years?'

'Yes, she was cremated two weeks ago, we'd been married sixty-eight years.'

Of course that's what he means – what an idiot I am! Well, I didn't know what to say except 'Oh, how are you getting on – how's it going?'

'Bloody horrible. I just wander the streets.' Oh dear, poor man.

At twenty past two I pack up as I need to be down where I was yesterday, to keep the appointment I have with the old man I said I'd give a guitar to – I've got it with me. I'm not 100% sure he'll turn up but I think he will – he certainly seems keen on learning. So, after a toilet and apple break I set up, tune up and he's here, in front of me, and again pointing, his finger almost touching my guitar string – 'So that's the first string, is it?'

'No, that's the sixth string, this one's the first string. Now, I've got your guitar with me… here it is.'

I take it out of the bag and hand it to him and show him an easy chord – a G major playing just four strings and fretting just one string. He gets it, after a fashion.

'Remember, try to fret just the strings you need to – don't let that finger touch the string next to it, or you won't hear that note…'

He thanks me. So, he's now got a guitar, a gigbag and I've even given him one of my picks – with Epiphone written on it. I'll leave the Chet Atkins thumbpick for the time being. So now he's all set – he can go home, get out his beginner's guitar books and learn.

'Good luck,' I say. 'Just keep at it!'

A woman about sixty-five says 'You remind me of Chet Baker, a famous American guitarist from the fifties and sixties.'

Chet Baker? I've heard the name but I thought he was a trumpet player, or something like that. I need to quiz her –

'Are you sure you don't mean Chet Atkins? *He* was a famous American guitarist in the fifties and sixties.' I'd also just played his arrangement of Ol' Man River! She *must* mean him, surely.

'No, Chet Baker.'

'Right, I thought he played the trumpet.'

She's not having it – 'No, not unless he had a career change.'

At home, I've been going through a tune for which I've had the music for a few years but I've never played it out here. It's the theme from The Deerhunter – Cavatina, the famous arrangement by John Williams. The only time I've played it was at the funeral of Fran's mum, in London a few months ago. Fran asked me to play Cavatina at the beginning of the service, along with Ave Maria, and at the end, when the people were leaving, she asked me to play Jesu, Joy of Man's Desiring. Which I did – I played it while everyone left the church and kept it going so that the people waiting to get in the cars to go to the crematorium would have some nice soothing background music. But as I didn't know how long anyone would be out there for, I kept playing it, over and over, for what seemed like ages, not knowing if there was anyone still there, outside. After awhile, Father Fergal put his head around the door and said 'You can stop playing now!' There was no one there – they'd all gone off! Anyway, for some reason, I've been reluctant to play Cavatina out here. Maybe I think it's so well-known and any mistake – and I'm bound to screw it up – will really stand out. Or maybe I feel it's not 'quirky' enough or maybe it's too serious sounding or maybe I don't really like it! Or maybe it's got something to do with the fact that *every* wedding guitar player does it. Whatever it is, I've decided to have a go... and I get a pound for my trouble from a man who actually saw the great John Williams play last night in Woking! – 'I was waiting for him to play the Asturias... what is it?'

'Leyenda.'

'Yeah, but he didn't play it,' he says.

And neither can I – it requires three good fingers on the right hand for the fast bits and I'm one short.

Later on, my French friend Marie-Thérèse visits. She loves the white dress in the shop near us – 'But it's too much, I buy all my clothes from charity shops, you know.'

So do I, I say – 'apart from my pants and socks, of course.'

She tells me about her neighbour, Bob – 'He has cancer, all over, but he never complains. He's cheerful and he's got nothing to be cheerful about.'

Earnings: £46.54

DAY 97   Sunday May 15th 2011
Winchester High Street, opposite WH Smiths
Time: 2:55-5:25pm

Busking on a Sunday is a rare occurrence for me – God and I rest on a Sunday. But an hour or two won't do any harm, I reckon. Emerging from the Westgate, I can already see quite a few people about, and when in town I take the by now obligatory patrol down the high street, to see who and what's about. Today the market, which is now on three days a week, is extended up to where the covered bit – The Pentice, begins. This means there's not as much busking area. There's a guy blowing a saxophone actually in one of the stalls. I reckon he must be the stall owner, and some sort of violin-y noise coming from a bit further down, where Bertie usually is. Apart from them, there's no one else playing anything, so I'm back up to WH Smiths, rather hurriedly in case someone turns up and gets the space – like those two girls the other day.

I set up near the grille where the pasty people dump their day's end sludge. In fact it's almost right in front of me, just to the left. This is because, due to my left hearing aid being lost, I need to have my amplifier on my right side, thereby moving myself further to the left, right near the pillar. There are many of these which support the roof all along this bit. I'm always next to a pillar! But I don't like to be in between two pillars as I'd be blocking the entire space from the high street to a shop like Boots or one of the others along there.

Maybe I think that, subconsciously, the pillar may take the place of another human, so I'm part of a duo and not so alone, not that I mind being alone – there's no discussions/arguments about what song to play, how long to play, when to take a break… Or maybe it's some sort of security blanket. Who knows… not me! However, the drain is quite pungent, I'll have to see how I get on.

The day turns out quite uneventful, and – unusually – barely anyone speaks to me. The money takes a long time coming and I end up with sixteen quid for two and a half hours – not good at all. I've had a lot worse, though. One interesting thing I've noticed out here is you sometimes get to see a different side to some people you may know. I've had people – acquaintances I've known for years and spoken to many times, ignore me when they see me out here. I think that all they see is a guy with a bucket, begging. They don't see someone very 'presentable' playing music, which has taken one heck of a long time to learn, and trying really hard to do it right. And although a lot of my acquaintances know of my busking and seem quite interested if I talk about it, when they see me actually doing it, some of them I don't think can handle it! I don't know – maybe they've never known a busker – I mean, it's not a 'proper job'! Although I bet I make as much an hour, or more, than some of them with their proper jobs do. I suppose it doesn't fit in to their closeted world. But they think they can walk past me and I won't see them – heaven forbid if someone else they know sees them in conversation with a guy with a bucket in front of him!

This happened today – someone was walking from one of the small roads which goes into the high street from the opposite side from where I am, so they were walking diagonally towards me. They obviously saw me rather late and tried to avoid me by going around the back of me, under the covered bit. I always see this sort of thing and I know what they're doing and sometimes I let it pass but sometimes I think they should know better and so make them uncomfortable by insisting they WILL acknowledge me! – so I shout 'Hi there!' and they don't like it! And a few days ago, I had someone come up and look down at my bucket the way you'd look at a dead animal that had been on the side of the road for a few days. Hm… yes, it's a kind of snobbery of which there is quite a lot of in Winchester. Maybe it's everywhere. I've also noticed, like Laurie Lee noticed when he was busking in the thirties, that well-off folks, or ones that *look* well-off, never ever 'give'. The lady who saw me just after she sold her house for £2 million I will regard as the exception to the rule! Still, she didn't give me much considering what she'd just got… but it's always the same – the ones who don't have much, they're the most generous. And the old people. Not the rich old people. And especially the women. The old women. But not the rich old women…

Earnings: £16.35

DAY 98   **Monday May 16th 2011**
             Winchester High Street, corner of Marks & Spencer
             Time: 1:30-6:05pm

One of my regulars, the man with two wives, turns up just after I start. What has he got to say for himself, the greedy man.

'Saw Lady Ga Ga on the telly last night. She's getting good, isn't she?'

'I don't know, I don't listen to that stuff,' I reply.

'No? I was thinking, she's as good as Madonna!'

'Well I don't like her, either – I never did.'

'No? Why's that? – Too commercial?'

'I don't know. I don't like music that sounds like it's made by a machine or a computer. I'm not into it.'

'Do you like other things, like Status Quo?'

'No, not really, it all sounds the same (I play a Quo-sounding thing for a few seconds)… there's no depth or anything! It's all right if you're at a party (which I never am), I suppose, and having a few drinks, maybe. I mean, it's good-time music, isn't it? But that's what it's supposed to be – you don't have to concentrate on it!'

'You're a very discerning man!' he says – the man who has to discern between two wives.

It's a long session – almost five hours, and all in one place. I keep promising myself (and everyone else) that I'll move to a different place in a minute but I never do it. Oh well, I may as well make the most of this spot now that it's out of bounds most days, due to the various markets taking over.

A couple in their late fifties walk by. The man says:

'Your D string needs tightening up a bit.'

The affront! 'Oh yeah, you reckon?' I shout.

'Yeah!' he shouts back.

The effrontery!… and the audacity!

'You serious?' I shout.

'What? yeah!' he replies, as he disappears around the corner. The cheek, the shameless audacity… and effrontery!

Another man, who's clearly had enough of me, walks by and says, 'Hello mate, you're always there, aren't you – playing a happy tune!' I'm not *always* here, though I am today – I'm beginning to feel I should be paying rent for this space. A couple down from Buxton give me some money. He's impressed with the toilets at the Abbey Gardens, nearby. They're the first toilets he's been in that have classical music playing in the background. That must be a new thing, I say, they never used to.

'So,' I ask, 'When are you going back?'

'Not for a few days – we've only just got here two hours ago. We're just having a look around the street. We'd like to find a nice restaurant.'

I say there's a Café Rouge somewhere, I think.

'No – we *know* what we like.'

A man comes up –

'Play some Chuck Berry, man! Yeah!' then *he* 'plays' some – Chuck Berry, I'm assuming – on his air guitar and sings an intro – 'Oh Carol…'

I'm happy to oblige and play the Chuck Berry intro everyone knows because they're all minor variations on the Johnny B Goode one.

'Yeah! All that stuff – it's the best… '

'Yeah, I don't play it much now,' I say, 'but I used to play all that when I was young. I played all that old stuff: Eddie Cochran, Buddy Holly, Chuck Berry, Carl Perkins, yep, all that stuff.'

'Hey, I'm forty-one and I still love it! Listen, I'm just going to Sainsbury's and I'll be back in a minute, OK?'

'Yeah, OK.' He never did come back.

My budding pensioner guitarist turns up at six o'clock. He's got a way of remembering the notes of the guitar strings – EADGBE.

'Now, let me think… it's an anagram… Ernie Ate Dynamite, Good-Bye Ernie.'

Earnings: £45.88

DAY 99   **Tuesday May 17th 2011**
               Winchester High Street
               1. Corner of Marks & Spencer. Time: 1:21-2:43pm
               2. Opposite WH Smiths. Time: 3:05-5:13pm

I pass Frank, accordioning in a spot I've not seen him at before, half-way down the high street, at the crossroads. He's (usually) always at the Buttercross or at the other end, at Marks & Spencer. A bit further down, I chat to Alan, my cheery septuagenarian street cleaner. At first I don't recognise him – he's in civilian clothes and sitting on a bench. I recognise his face, though. He's always smiling. Always. I find out why he's not wearing his work gear and also why I haven't seen him for a few days. He's just retired. He says he is to go to the hospital for quite a serious operation tomorrow and his boss has let him go early. He says he'll miss the social side of his job – he certainly must know a lot about everyone on the street, I reckon. He says he's waiting for his wife, then there's a high pitched noise: it's her phoning him and a minute later she's here. I say 'so long' and I hope the operation goes well.

'Oh well, they can only do what they can,' he says.

A great guy – always friendly, always!

Alan the street cleaner

I can see Frank's taking a break so I go and say hello. We make a deal – I'll go and do a bit down at the corner and if he gets bored he can come down later and we'll switch places.

I have a fairly peaceful session, in that I'm not bombarded with too many interruptions – well meant or not. Four schoolboys stand in front of me. They don't speak, but I guess (correctly – possibly because they don't speak) that they're French. One at a time they come forward to give me some shrapnel. Then, three drift off, leaving one. He still doesn't speak to me. After two minutes I ask him his name. It's François.

'How old are you, François?'

Twelve years old, he says. Blue eyes, a lot of freckles. He asks if I can play any blues or Sweet Home Chicago – how does a twelve-year-old French kid know about that stuff?! I reel off a fast Eric Clapton blues-y 'lick', as we used to say in the seventies, then try and convert him to the Chet Atkins way of thinking. He sits down beside me on my right with his legs crossed and stays there for fifteen minutes. A few people walk past and smile at me. One lady says 'Is he with you?' and laughs. It's like Frank with his dog – I've got this freckled French kid! His friends walk to and fro a few times and eventually he joins them. Au revoir, François.

I attempt Vincent today... and really mess it up but a lady comes around the corner. I get this often – I'll finish something and someone will appear and say they've been listening from just around the corner, like at the bus stop maybe. She gives me a pound, which I feel bad about considering my botched performance, so I apologise for making a load of mistakes – 'Thank you... and sorry!'

A bit later Frank turns up – he must have got bored, and drinks his cup of coffee on the bench across from me. I do a few more songs then pack up, have a break, eat my apple then I'm off up the road... My well-dressed, well-spoken regular drops by – 'I'm sorry again, I haven't got a sous to give you!' To another man, I mention that it's my birthday today. He says I should have this written on a hat – I'd get more money. Maybe, but blatant opportunism – it just isn't my style, I say! Well, not usually.

Another regular, the old guy now in possession of one of my guitars turns up and I'm not sure if he was trying to avoid me but he seemed to be going round the back of me, so I wouldn't see him. Well, it's no good! I stop him and ask how he's getting on with the guitar. He says his fingers won't stretch to do a C chord shape. Hmm... I give him my guitar to see how he's doing it and it's all wrong and he looks like he's in pain – it's painful enough just to watch.

'Your fingers need to be at an angle to the guitar neck, you're coming in straight on, you need to angle your wrist, about twenty degrees...'

He tries it, it's a bit better. Having played the guitar for a hundred years, I suppose I take this sort of thing for granted. It must be a real challenge for someone that age who hasn't ever held a guitar before. I must have patience...

I get a compliment from a lady – 'You're getting better!'

'Well, thanks! It helps that it's not freezing cold any more. It's a lot easier to play when it's warmer.'

'Hmm... you must be practicing, too.'

'Practice? I do enough of that out here!'

As I'm packing away my stuff, Frank turns up and the dog, Kazoo, is trying to get at a pigeon which is on the ground, obviously wounded – as Frank says 'It mustn't be able to fly or else it would have, with the dog trying to get it. I'd finish it off but there's too many people about.'

I'm curious – 'How would you do that?'

'Strangle it.'

'You'd strangle a pigeon?'

'Yeah, put it out of its misery.'

'Hm... yeah, I suppose.'

Earnings: £39.00

DAY 100

Wednesday May 18th 2011
Hungerford Foot Bridge, London
Time: 1:45-4pm

A landmark day – my hundredth, which finishes in an appropriately memorable way. My session up here in the Big Smoke – the second in as many weeks, was due to my attendance at the unveiling of a restored statue of Frydyric Chopin, which took place in the morning, outside the Royal Festival Hall. Also present are: The Duke Of Gloucester (KG, GCVO, no less) – the statue's unveiler, The Polish Ambassador – Ms Barbara Tuge-Erecińska, a member of the British Government who looks like every other male member of the British Government, and a couple of hundred other, mainly quite well-off, aged English and Poles including a lady, very tall with big orange hair, she's wearing a green velvet dress/coat... surely it can't be, can it? is it?... it *is* – it's Rula Lenska!

There is also a small band playing a selection of early-twentieth-century American jazz, one tune being a medley – Echoes Of Harlem, the connection with mid-nineteenth-century piano music escaping my comprehension. After the unveiling there is a Chopin recital in the nearby Purcell Room by Alexander Ardakov, who returns for two encores, the first being the famous so-called 'Raindrop' prelude – Opus 28, No 15. He plays it better than me.

After the recital there is a VIP reception. A man makes an announcement – 'for those with tickets with a gold trim who *know* you're going to the reception, please leave the hall first. For those with a gold trim who aren't sure if you're invited, you're not!' Ms Lenska is invited. I am not.

My plan is to now do a spot of busking on the nearby Hungerford Foot Bridge – to make or try to make back as much of my train fare as I can. I've seen buskers here in the past and there's always a constant stream of people walking across. At the top of the steps, the Big Issue seller sees my guitar and says:

'Ye goin' to de a bit o buskin', yeah? Jes de it? Ye carry on! Lots o gid buskin' here, pal, ye carry on!'

'OK, thanks!' I walk on past the centre of the bridge and set up, nearer the side where the Embankment Underground station is, facing east with a nice view of St. Pauls and to my right, the Festival Hall, where I've just been. I've got my back to the train bridge, which is right next to this footbridge. I'm wearing a suit and tie because statue unveiling is a serious affair but decide to take my tie off, as I don't want to look posh – people might not give me money.

I set up and go to it and, like many times, the money's slow to start and I feel a bit self-conscious, especially in a suit, but after fifteen minutes it starts coming in, steadily. It's mainly tourists crossing the bridge, stopping to take photos of each other in really silly poses. They'll be doing this and hearing me and if they like it, they'll come over and give me a pound. There are also quite a few business men/women. No money from them. I also see many of those who were at the unveiling/recital. I know they were there because they're all carrying the free programme we were all given. None of them give me anything – not even a look, apart from one man with his wife –

'I like your music!' he says.

Thank you, posh man – appreciator of not only Romantic-era piano music but also of 1950s Travis fingerstyle guitar.

I meet a few people, including Roberto, a Flamenco guitarist who loves my Chet Atkins stuff and a little Indian girl who comes up and says 'where's the princess?' over and over for some reason I'll never know. 'You play tunes!' says a lady... 'nice bit of echo(reverb, actually)' says a man. I play more or less non-stop, and mainly a very small selection – The Third Man, La Vie En Rose, Ol' Man River, Mr. Sandman and Yellow Bird. But it doesn't matter – there's no one in any shops or on benches to get bored!

The noise bothers me a bit – there's a lot! – I've got the trains behind me, the pleasure boats honking away underneath and all these helicopters going over. At one point there are two trains coming in, a boat and a helicopter. But the money's pretty steady and I cream off ten pound coins just in case someone tries to liberate them, and put them in my pocket.

There're a few left so it's going OK – I've been here two and a half hours... but it all comes to an end at four o'clock.

'I'm sorry, I really like what you're playing (it's Deve Ser Amor, first performance) and it's not too loud but I have to ask you to stop.'

It's a short man in a uniform and cap. It's a PCSO – here on the Hungerford Bridge!

He apologises again, and again he likes what I play but no one's allowed to play in a public thoroughfare in the City of Westminster – no they're not, not without a permit. I ask if I can get one from him. No, he says I have to contact the local council about that, like they have to do if they want to play at Covent Garden.

So that's that. I don't mind really – I've done over two hours and I know I've made most of the train fare back. And this guy's quite friendly and asks about the stuff I play and how long I've been playing – 'About two hours before you turned up!' I say. He has to be seen doing his job – there's a CCTV camera somewhere near recording all this, he says. I say I didn't know you couldn't busk here – I'm from Winchester, you don't need a permit there (yet). He has to write me out a ticket and I have to tell him my name and address, then where it says SEARCH GROUNDS, he writes, MALE WAS SEEN PLAYING HIS GUITAR ON THE HUNGERFORD BRIDGE. MALE WAS ADVISED. SATISFACTORY STOP.

I write down *his* name, too. It's Ali – his last name. His first is too long for his name badge, he says, and he's number 7836 CW – City of Westminster. Ali apologises again, and while we're talking about busking – he says it's a shame as a lot of people think the buskers give a bit of colour to London – a man walks by and drops a pound in the bucket – 'in protest!' he says.

So that's the end of that. I pack up and take a stroll up to the West End, first to the police station near Charing Cross to ask about this permit business. At the information counter, Constable Plod doesn't know about it –

'Hmm, maybe that's why I haven't seen any buskers lately,' he thinks.

'Well, you would have seen *me* half an hour ago if you were walking across the Hungerford Bridge, until one of your PCSOs turned up.'

'Hmm, your best bet is try the local council – they're all different for all the areas. Hmmm.'

'OK, thanks.'

After that, I go looking for a proper gig, some place that will have a solo guitarist. There are hundreds of bars and restaurants around here, there must be some place. Some very tall guy named Tyrone in one place I went seemed interested, although he said something like 'What would be your deal – would you want paying?' Deary me.

I go to a few more places but my guitar and amp bag are getting heavy and I've had enough of this so I make my way back via Trafalgar Square, where I see a guy busking with his violin over a backing track in front of the National Gallery. I wait until he's finished his Aria then asked him if he's had any hassle from the local constabulary. No, he hasn't. I look the other way and see about ten police men/women looking over the concrete wall at a demonstration, something about Sri Lanka. None of them are bothered about this guy, and there is another street 'performer' near him, all painted in bronze, dressed up like Wyatt Earp, standing on a small plinth. I reckon it's just the PCSOs who hassle the buskers – the real police don't care! It starts to rain so I make my way back to Waterloo, over the bridge, past the place where I was busted earlier and back home to count my money. Turns out I was just forty-five pence short of making back my train fare, so 'mission accomplished'… almost.

Earnings: £30.05

Albums by Marvin B. Naylor

Monsters and Mad Things (2004)
The Last Flight of Billy Balloon (2008)
The Stargazer's Symphonium (2011)
Earth and All the Universes (2014)
The Spiral Sky (2017)

www.marvinbnaylor.com

Lightning Source UK Ltd.
Milton Keynes UK
UKHW041830120722
405753UK00004B/329

9 781908 011893